P9-CJF-035

A WOMAN'S GUIDE TO A SIMPLER LIFE

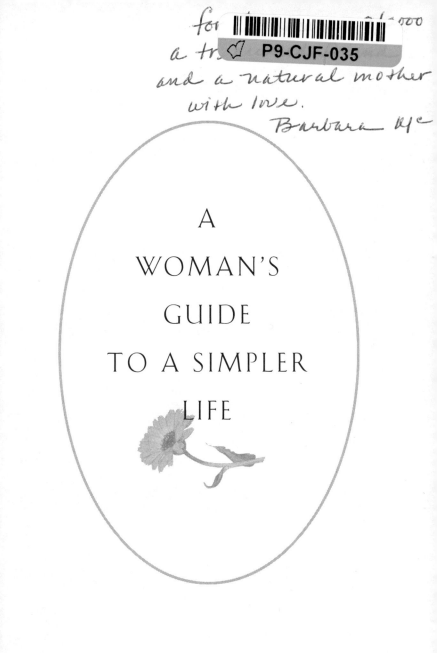

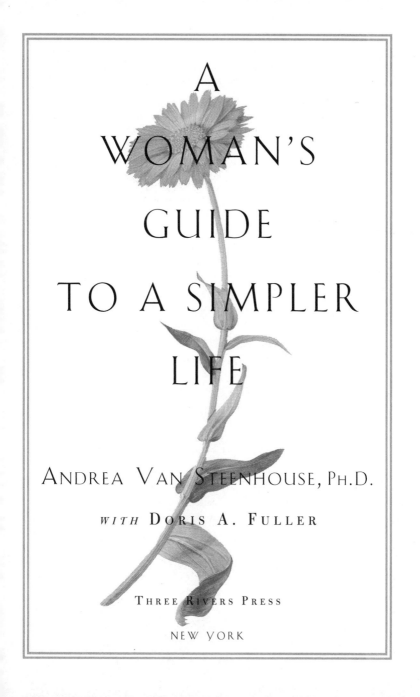

A WOMAN'S GUIDE TO A SIMPLER LIFE

ANDREA VAN STEENHOUSE, Ph.D.

WITH DORIS A. FULLER

THREE RIVERS PRESS

NEW YORK

Published by Three Rivers Press, a division of Crown Publishers, Inc.,
201 East 50th Street, New York, New York 10022.
Member of the Crown Publishing Group.

Originally published in hardcover by Harmony Books in 1996.

First paperback edition printed in 1997.

Random House, Inc. New York, Toronto, London, Sydney, Auckland
www.randomhouse.com

THREE RIVERS PRESS and colophon are trademarks
of Crown Publishers, Inc.

Printed in the United States of America

Design by Lynne Amft

Library of Congress Cataloging-in-Publication Data
Van Steenhouse, Andrea.
A woman's guide to a simpler life /
by Andrea Van Steenhouse; with Doris A. Fuller
Originally published: New York : Harmony Books © 1996.
1. Women—Conduct of life. 2. Simplicity. 3. Women—Life skills
guides. I. Fuller, Doris A. II. Title.
BJ1610.V36   1997   158.1'082—dc21   97–23755

ISBN 0-609-80145-7

10 9 8 7 6 5 4 3

To

BOB ELLIOTT

Brother, friend, rainmaker

ACKNOWLEDGMENTS

Many lives touched mine in ways that significantly contributed to this book. There are several friends on whose help I particularly relied. Dr. Dianne Singleton provided insightful suggestions and thoughtful comments; her warmth, wisdom, and friendship enrich my life. Mary Beth Starzel's support, willingness to listen, and constant good cheer were abundant and helpful.

Margaret Maupin offered early and steadfast enthusiasm. Jody Rein saw the possibilities and gently guided the polishing of ideas. Our editor, Shaye Areheart, shined her light on this project from the very beginning and remained a spirited advisor throughout. Thanks also to the invisible hands at Crown who worked with such a light and sensitive touch.

I owe an extraordinary debt to everyone who called my radio show and generously shared their stories. I thank them for helping me come to know and understand the resilience of the human spirit.

I am fortunate to have parents and siblings with whom I can share the joys of connection. To my husband, Pat, and sons Jim, John, and Michael, I appreciate your good-hearted permission to allow me to use your lives in examples, and thank you for your precious ability to help me remember what matters.

~ *Andrea Van Steenhouse*

The image of the writer feverishly creating while locked away in her solitary room belies the inestimable role of the family, friends, and key colleagues. These are among mine.

Nora Jacob, boon companion and librarian extraordinaire,

was ever available with her friendship, her expertise, and her cybersurfboard. Jeanette DeWyze tirelessly answered publishing questions and ran interference for me elsewhere in my world. Margaret Maupin provided the critical first nudge, Jody Rein set the course, and Shaye Areheart waited for this work with a conviction and enthusiasm I will always cherish.

My writer's room would not exist were it not for the support of Don Fuller, whose faith in me seems to know no limits. Its solitude would be intolerable without my children, Greg and Natalie, who stand just beyond the threshold (and sometimes inside) with their noisy cheers and boisterous love.

Doris A. Fuller

CONTENTS

A
WOMAN'S
GUIDE
TO A SIMPLER
LIFE

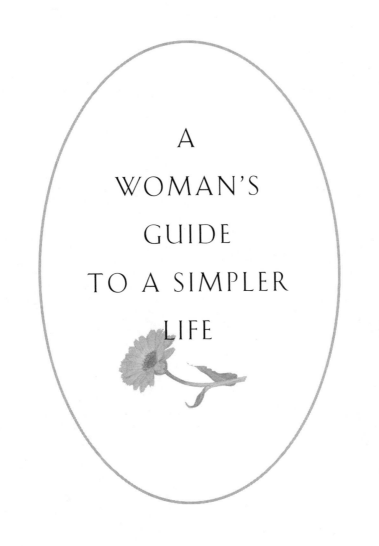

INTRODUCTION

One summer vacation a few years ago, a close friend and I kissed our husbands good-bye, loaded our children into the car and set off for a rented lake cottage. For the week that followed, we experienced one of those magical summer adventures full of blue skies and lazy days, our schedules dictated by nothing more than our basic needs and our whims.

Among our greatest joys, we soon agreed, was the sheer simplicity of our time. There were no phones, no jobs, no possessions to maintain. We had no worldly goods with us but our clothes, and a good-sized suitcase could contain them all.

Each day, we rose, dressed, ate, and then pursued whatever activity exerted the greatest pull on our spirits—a swim, a walk to the ice-cream store, a search for familiar constellations in the clear skies. At the end of our stay, we all piled back in the car, tanned, rested, and snug in the satisfaction of how serenely we had passed the week.

Our route home was equally leisurely. When it took us through a small Amish community where we had been told we could find a superb craftsman willing to show his handcrafted furniture to outsiders, we determined to find him. The fact that our directions were vague and his door was unmarked only added to the mystique. We felt we were hunting hidden treasure as we wound through the streets of the town until we found the house that matched our instructions. Kids at our heels, we knocked at the door.

The man who answered was on the near side of middle age, perhaps a little reserved but certainly gracious. When we asked to see his furniture, he promptly invited us all in, and we stepped through the door into the living room of his home.

Dianne and I were immediately stunned.

The room into which we walked was both more bare and more beautiful than any we could remember. It held little furniture, only essentials, and each piece was as simple as the hands of a man could make them. The wooden floors were uncarpeted and worn to a rich sheen. If there was ornamentation, it was not to be seen in the shadows; no electricity lit this space.

As he led us to his workshop and shared with us his work, our host spoke in words that were sparing but kind, and we sensed the same clean spirit in his soul that we saw in his dwelling.

Driving away, we were both silent for several miles. We had achieved one level of simplicity on our vacation getaway. The Amish woodworker had shown us another. In the pure light of both, the lives waiting to engulf us back home seemed needlessly complex.

My home will never look like our woodworker's Amish home; I could not live so sparely. But the simplicity I tasted within his walls stimulated a hunger inside me for the same simplicity in my own life.

On our trip, Dianne and I had temporarily simplified our outer lives. In the home of the Amish follower, we witnessed the simplicity possible when we allow all that surrounds us to be dictated by our hearts.

Not many women today live simple lives. We are workers, mothers, wives, daughters, friends, kin-keepers, hostesses, volunteers, and many other things to many people. We are overworked and overwhelmed. We are tired.

Some of us have studied time management manuals or bought the books on organizing our lives. We have tried a hundred steps to a simpler life. Nothing has helped.

I believe that's because we haven't begun at the beginning, with knowing what we cherish most certainly in our hearts. In our innocence, we become consumed by connections that matter little . . . but demand much.

I suspect that if each of us could walk through the door of that Amish home, where the heartbeat of the craftsman echoes in every corner, we might all be inspired to search our own hearts and bring our lives into concert with them.

Because we can't, I have written this book.

I have a word of caution for fellow seekers.

Simplicity looks different in different lives because each heart holds its own themes. It looks different at different times of our own lives because our tempos change with age, events, and experience.

Simplicity is not a matter of time management or efficiency or organization. It does not consist of shedding one set of life furnishings in order to make room for another. Rather, a simpler life is one in which the knowledge of what matters dictates all that surrounds us. It is a life lived with the courage to let go of what our hearts know does not belong. It is a more balanced life, not a more expert balancing act.

What you will find here is not a bookful of *answers* but a bookful of *questions,* not a *formula* but the *makings* you may want to consider as you compose your own simpler life. The suggestions, and there are many, are merely that, no more.

There is no right or wrong in the search for simplicity. It is not a destination, like a house we move into, but a direction, like the path that leads toward the house. Where it takes us, if we dare to follow, is back to our hearts.

May this book be your compass.

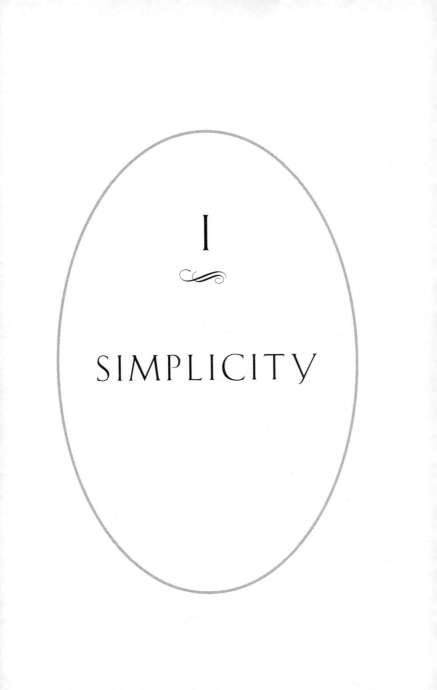

I

SIMPLICITY

D O
I N E E D
T O
S I M P L I F Y ?

Few of us awaken one morning with the sudden realization that our lives have grown too complicated. Rather, awareness steals over us as our days become more full and less fulfilling.

Our spirits are disturbed with a restless longing—a sense of yearning coupled with a melancholy that whatever we are missing is somehow out of reach.

I heard this longing in the voices of women who called the radio talk show I hosted for many years.

> *I'm married to the man I love, I have wonderful*
> *kids and a great job, **but** . . .*

And there they are, the words that are flesh to the longings:

- I don't feel close to anyone, even my mate.

- I long for traditions, but they don't bring me much joy.

- *I don't have any* or *I don't get enough* are words I often use when I speak of sleep, recreation, leisure.

- I never have time for the friends who mean the most to me.

- My work seems to run my life.

- Every request feels urgent whether it's important or not.

- No matter what I'm doing, part of me is somewhere else— when I'm at work, I'm thinking about my children; when I'm with the children, I'm preoccupied with work.

- Home is not a haven but another place to labor.

- Technology feels like a trap—my heart sinks every time I see the light blinking on the telephone-answering machine.

- I use alcohol, drugs, or food to get me through my days or nights.

Underlying these words is the awareness that after years of accumulating and pushing the envelope of our potential, after trying so hard to make a mark and accomplish as much as possible, we are surprised and confused to find ourselves asking . . .

Why? To what end?

How do we know if we need to simplify?

In truth, if this book has found its way into your hands— if you bought it, borrowed it, received it as a gift—you already know.

You live with the frenzy, the weariness, the emptiness, the hunger. You have looked into the garden of your life and found a thicket of weeds.

My friend Kris sums up her own ache for a simpler life by saying she wants to chop more wood and carry more water.

We know we need to simplify when we share her ache.

I have everything I ever dreamed possible. But where is the balance?

9

~ JONI TOMASETTI
   Wife, mother, artist, flight attendant

IS IT TIME?

As I was preparing to write this book, I described it to a young woman engaged in a desperate juggling act with a high-profile career, young marriage, and new child.

"You're not going to say I have to eliminate anything, are you?" she asked with an anxiety so acute that I sensed panic at its edges.

I could read on her face that she was not ready for what I needed to say.

It is possible to feel pressured and drained and over-whelmed and yet, like this young woman, not be ready to sim-plify. We do not all find ourselves ready at the same point in our lives; some of us never feel ready at all.

Yet as we rush through our busy days, many of us do en-counter signs that the time has come to listen more carefully to our hearts. When we do, we find:

. . . that our spirits are more often dissatisfied than contented.

. . . that our longing for a different life is keener than our drive to maintain the one we currently live.

. . . that we are willing to rethink relationships and activities and habits we long assumed were unalterable.

When we go to the optometrist to have our eyes examined, she flips a host of images before us and asks:

> *Clearer or fuzzier?*
> *Clearer or fuzzier?*
> *Clearer or fuzzier?*

Being ready for a simpler life implies that we are willing to hold up every choice, past and present, and consider whether it grows clearer or fuzzier when viewed in the light of what we hold most dear.

The strength of any plan is in the timing.

CHARLES-LOUIS DE SECONDAT
MONTESQUIEU
French philosopher

HOW DO
I
START?

I began my own efforts to simplify with my kitchen drawers.

I was fresh from my trip with Dianne and the children and still mightily impressed with the essential simplicity of the cottage we had rented and the house of the Amish craftsman. I returned home and cleaned out all my kitchen drawers, buying new silverware holders and neatly arranging all the flatware.

Next, I moved on to wooden tabletops. I wanted to leave them exposed, as the woodworker had done, so I put away everything that wasn't absolutely necessary. I even tried to find a furniture polish that would fill my rooms with the same scent that filled the craftsman's.

My efforts gave me an immediate visual comfort. I could open my kitchen drawers or look around my living room and experience a distinct sense of satisfaction, even peace.

I had begun to simplify my life.

* * *

When I am asked, *How do I start simplifying?* I answer, *Start where you can.*

There is no road map to a simpler life. Each of us starts from a different point and follows a different route. And none of us ever "arrives."

Simplifying life is not a project we can schedule, perform, and complete before going on to the next. It is an approach, a habit of taking care that the choices we make, small and large, harmonize with our hearts.

You don't have to know your heart in order to start, but you will know it better as soon as you begin. Choices define and reveal. They are like the numbers you dial on a combination lock; when they are the right ones, you hear a click and know the tumblers have fallen into place.

A choice that rewards you with a sense of harmony between yourself and what surrounds you reveals something you value. A choice that leaves you feeling empty, or worse—annoyed, resentful, sorrowful—indicates you're under the influence of something other than what truly matters.

Let's say, in a burst of housecleaning, you pitch all the letters you saved from your college days. Whether you wake up the next day with a sense of relief that you've put the past behind you or find yourself digging through the trash to pull them back out, you have learned something about what matters to you.

As you pass through this book, you will encounter options that seem powerful and inviting and options that seem frivolous and dull. Both will inform you about the landscape of your own soul.

While we each start simplifying in a different place, it does seem sensible to start where we have a chance for success. Who would choose to learn to ski on ice?

So I do suggest you begin by thinking of every corner of life where there is clutter and then picking *one* where you stand a fighting chance of conquest.

For me, this was the kitchen drawers. Another woman might start by contacting one of those clearinghouses that make sure you don't receive junk mail, or by canceling the "call waiting" function on the telephone, or by reshuffling the assignment of family duties.

Wherever you choose to start, remember that simplifying your life is neither a job nor a test. There is no such thing as perfection. You don't have to do this overnight.

Even *thinking* about simplifying your life represents progress. What seems unimaginable today will seem inevitable on some future day.

Start where you can.

Start where you must.

Just start.

> *Courage is the price that life exacts for granting peace.*
>
> AMELIA EARHART
> American aviator

HEARTSONGS
AND OTHER
HIDING PLACES

The glorious beauty of tuning our lives to our hearts is that we don't have to invent anything. We don't have to *find* something to matter to us. Most everything we value is already there, perhaps in hiding, but in place.

The routes back to what matters are innumerable. I offer three that I have used to find my own.

We can listen for our *heartsongs.*

Heartsongs are the common themes that run through our lives, the impulses and longings that are the undercurrent beneath the surface.

The heartsong that reawakened in the Amish woodworker's home was my yearning for open space. Open spaces help me feel at peace; closed ones feel claustrophobic.

This is a minor heartsong, not nearly as powerful as the one of family or friends, but it still resonates. Many qualities in the craftsman's life could have spoken to me—his calm manner, the absence of invasive technology—but order was the one I claimed first.

Similar themes weave through each of our lives. We know them when a person, a sight, an experience, a sensation tugs at our spirits as if to say, *This way . . . come this way.* It's what we feel when we walk past a bed spilling over with new blooms and wish our own were as well tended.

Our themes are beyond number, and each woman has a set as individual as a fingerprint. A heartsong can be as simple as a passion for needlework or as profound as the desire for a child. They are alike only in that they have the ability to help us rediscover what we value. When we hear them and honor them, it is more likely that the choices we make will be anchored in what matters.

This book is full of places to listen for the themes of our hearts—in our minds, our homes, our jobs, our families, our friendships, our traditions. Finding even one is like polishing a single pair of shoes in the closet; it gives us a new standard by which to judge all the rest.

Never underestimate the power of a small beginning. I've given space in this book to clothes and parents, cooking and children, friends and exercise. Clearly, the significance of each of these is not equal. Yet the *impact* of simplifying any one of them may be the same. *Any* completed step toward simplicity renews our spirits and builds our confidence to take another.

After I had cleaned out my kitchen drawers and cleared my

tabletops, I saw a dozen other things that were taking up space in my life without adding any meaning. Honoring just one small heartsong tuned my ear to those that hummed in other, more significant places.

The reward for our first small steps toward simplicity is the courage to attempt bigger ones.

When I was about nineteen, I spent a week in Alabama visiting with my uncle Andy and his family. One afternoon, I was thumbing through my aunt's magazines when I came across an article by two women recalling their lifelong friendship.

What struck me as I read their story were the anecdotes about all the trips they had taken and all the times they had sped past a tempting stop with the promise "on the way back." Then they never went back. I was so moved by the regret their choices had caused them that I vowed never to pass a turning in my travels.

Life being what it is, I have passed many turnings since then. My self-promise, so heartfelt at the time, seems hopelessly naive in the present. Even so, the insight of that moment on my uncle's porch still serves me. It reminds me of something that mattered before what mattered had so much to compete with, and it keeps me from passing *all* the turnings.

Life bestows on each of us *gifts of a moment,* instants when what we value is crystal clear and unclouded.

Some of these come in the exuberant preadolescent years when we don't wonder who we are, we just *are,* full of ourselves and our dreams. Others come to us as teenagers or young adults when we *endlessly* wonder who we are. Many of the most memorable ones come to us in times of hardship or tragedy.

In the intensity of these moments, we often resolve to live by the insights that have been revealed. Then, as I did when I left my uncle's home, we get on with the business of living and forget.

As we set out to simplify our lives, we are wise to sift through our memories for as many of these past moments as we can find and to be alert to new ones as they come along. Their clarity gives us a mirror for our souls.

Patterns—how we behave and how we react to the behavior of others—are clues to what matters to us. If we can learn to stand back and watch for patterns, we may rediscover the values we have misplaced.

WE CAN WATCH OURSELVES.

If everything in our lives goes on hold when a loved one's birthday dawns, we know that rituals matter. If our household is incomplete without a dog or a cat, even though we're allergic to both, we know that pets matter. Observing ourselves with a watchful spirit can teach us much.

WE CAN NOTE WHAT WE ADMIRE IN OTHERS.

When we find ourselves drawn to another person, it may be that we have discovered a quality we wish for ourselves. Just as I did by copying the Amish woodworker, many of us begin simplifying by replicating what we admire in someone else.

WE CAN NOTICE WHAT WE DISLIKE IN OTHERS.

When the way another person carries on her life disturbs us, we may have found an unpleasant reflection of ourselves. Considering whether the habit that troubles us has a twin in our own lives helps us find some of the pieces that don't belong.

> *There is an internal landscape, a geography of the*
> *soul; we search for its outlines all our lives.*

~○ JOSEPHINE HART
British novelist

RITUAL

One of the first obstacles we face when we begin to simplify is the habit of making choices without checking them out with our hearts. What we need is a Ritual of Pause. In place of our habit of adding without pause, we need to practice pausing before we add.

An acquaintance calls and suggests lunch. Before agreeing, you pause and consider . . . *Is this someone with whom I want to spend a rare, prized lunch hour?*

The school calls and says it is desperate for volunteers to staff the annual carnival. Before answering, you pause and reflect . . . *Can I take on this obligation without spreading myself too thin?*

The boss calls you in and offers you an exciting new assignment that requires a higher level of commitment. Before accepting, you pause and contemplate . . . *Will I be able to maintain a balanced life if my hours are longer and my responsibilities greater?*

It doesn't matter if at first you still find yourself unable to answer with a firm *No*. Respond with a pause, and you give *No* room to grow.

II

SIMPLIFYING
OUR INNER
LIFE

GREAT
EXPECTATIONS

I know a gracious hostess who prides herself on the meals she makes for loved ones in her own kitchen. For many years, she entertained according to her own set of unwritten rules, including one that said nothing could be served unless she prepared it with her own hands. No matter how large the crowd, how heavy the chores, how distracting the competing obligations, she personally chopped, stirred, garnished, and served each and every dish.

To the woman's utter dismay, a day arrived when a dinner party was planned and the guests were expected. Then the electricity went out during her prime kitchen hours. She was left with two options: She could serve a meal she hadn't prepared, or she could cancel the party.

Deciding that prefabricated food was the lesser of two evils, she rushed to a local discount warehouse and purchased a frozen lasagna, threw it in the oven, and served it with garlic bread, green salad, and apologies to the assembled guests.

Who, of course, were having a wonderful time and couldn't have cared less.

The woman *expected* to personally prepare every course, but her expectation was an orphan, unshared and unconnected to anybody else at the dinner table. We, her guests, were simply glad for her warmth and the cheer of good company; the food, even though it was delicious, was a sociable side dish.

We build our lives on a foundation of expectations bestowed upon us first by parents and later by teachers, peers, employers, spouses, offspring, community, and a host of others, including ourselves. Then we get on with the business of living the rest of our lives, and we never go back to check for cracks.

Some of our expectations are useful: Our teachers expect us to work up to our abilities; we see ourselves reflected in their eyes, and we live up to their assumptions. A playmate assures us that we can swim all the way across the swimming pool; we believe her and overcome our fears. Our parents expect us to finish our education so we can support ourselves; we do and are better off for it.

Other expectations prove to be more questionable: attending every single Little League game of the season, chipping in for the fourth wedding gift of the year for a coworker we hardly know, being available to a struggling friend on the night we need to get to bed early.

The problem with expectations is not that they exist. Expectations are absolutely necessary to the functioning of society. When I drive down a highway, I expect to stay on my side of the road, and I expect you to stay on yours. Both of us fulfill this expectation because we are members of an ordered society, and we both survive as a result.

The problem with expectations arises when we don't distinguish the necessary from the unnecessary, the realistic from the unrealistic, the important from the I-could-really-live-without-this. We allow assumptions—someone's, *anyone's,* or own own—to evolve into habits that we perform without stopping to ask . . .

> *Who thought this up?*

Simplifying our lives, even in a single narrow area, requires examining the expectations that motivate us and asking ourselves . . .

> *Why am I doing this?*
> *Is this necessary?*
> *Is it important to me?*
> *Why is it important?*

Unexamined expectations all feel like five-alarm fires that require our immediate, complete attention. Looked at more closely, it turns out that some are genuinely compelling but others are faulty smoke detectors.

My friend Rose used to handle the seating assignments for the huge fund-raiser her favorite charity staged every year. Nobody else was ever asked to take on the job; it was just expected that Rose would do it even though it required countless hours and inevitably ended up with someone griping about his or her seating, no matter how meticulous she was.

One year, when the weight of the job seemed to be particularly heavy, I asked, "Why do you do this year after year when it no longer brings you much satisfaction?"

Rose was stumped. She had never stopped to examine the expectation and whether it still held meaning for her. She had not asked herself . . .

What am I getting out of this?
What is it costing me?
Is it worth the price?

Once she answered these questions, the priority of this particular expectation took a new place.

It is hard to question expectations because we seem to breathe them in with the air, and they feel just as natural. And questioning expectations is merely the first and easiest step. If we are going to simplify our inner lives, we may need to reject the questionable ones.

I have found several successful tactics that may be used alone or in almost any combination to loosen the hold of flawed expectations.

1. YOU CAN GIVE YOURSELF PERMISSION TO LET GO.

Once you can face an expectation and say, *I don't have to do this,* it loses a great deal of its power. Once Rose realized, *I am knocking myself out for this event because I'm expected to, even though I've already served for a long time and many others could do the job equally well,* the reign of this particular expectation was doomed.

2. YOU CAN GET LUCKY.

For the hostess, it took serving a frozen lasagna to her guests and discovering that they still enjoyed her hospitality before she could say, *I don't have to cook every dish from scratch in order to give a successful dinner party.* Sometimes fortune does the hard work for you, giving you an unsought opportunity to learn that the expectation didn't matter much to begin with.

3. You can pretend.

Vince Lombardi was right: The best defense is a good offense. You don't have to wait for fortune's helping hand. You can find out on your own whether expectations matter by imagining, *What will happen if I don't do this?*

This starts with a little talk with yourself:

> *What will happen if I go into the Monday morning staff meeting (where I'm the only woman) and don't volunteer (as everyone expects) to keep the minutes?*
>
> *Habits and expectations die hard; if I don't volunteer, I can expect to be asked.*
>
> *So I can say, "I'd really like to concentrate on the discussion without taking notes today."*
>
> *What will happen?*
>
> *They will be disappointed, and I may feel uncomfortable at first. I can live with that.*
>
> *I won't cave in at the first sign of opposition—or the next one. This is not a catastrophe.*

The knowledge that the sun still rises the morning after you say good-bye to an expectation is wonderfully reassuring.

4. You can tell the world.

Announcements are a way to lower the expectations of those around you.

One colleague's telephone message says, "Because of the volume of calls we receive, I am unlikely to personally return each one. If you would like a response, please send a fax with all the information we need to begin to help you." Not surprisingly, he doesn't get many phone messages.

There are other ways to ease out of expectations, but I have found few as swift and effective as an announcement.

It takes courage to reject others' expectations, because somebody will be disappointed. You can hardly expect the kids to cheer when they find they have to pack their own lunches. If your self-worth depends on keeping everybody's approval and you do something that generates disapproval, you're temporarily at risk for self-doubt.

Take heart. Most of us hit the road to a simpler life after years of forgetting or overlooking what is important to us. The first excursions are the hardest.

> *It is hard to fight an enemy who has outposts in your mind.*
>
> SALLY KEMPTON
> American writer

A
GIRL SCOUT
IS
RESPONSIBLE

One of the most overwhelming aspects of modern life is that we seem to have more responsibilities than we can easily manage.

This is not an illusion.

We do.

In her landmark book on working mothers, *The Second Shift,* Arlie Hochschild noted that when the time women spend on their paid jobs is added with the time they spend on housework and child care, women work roughly fifteen hours more each week than men. Over the period of a year, this adds up to an extra month of twenty-four-hour days.

Nonmothers fare a little better on the home front because they don't have to deal with child-rearing issues, but they're still pulling longer shifts than their male counterparts. What's more, they're finding themselves pulled into additional activities precisely because they're viewed as having more available time.

Indeed, it's hard to pick up a women's magazine or a lifestyle section of the newspaper without coming across another depressing infobit:

- Thirty-eight percent of Americans *always* feel rushed . . . and women feel more rushed than men.

- American women average 10.7 hours of each waking day caring for their preschoolers; American men average less than an hour.

- Women are spending more years of their lives at work than ever before.

Each new revelation tightens the noose a little more.

Responsibilities are real. Expectations are what we or someone else thinks we *ought* to do; responsibilities are what we or someone else *has* to do. For example, we may *choose* to serve home-cooked meals instead of fast food because of an *expectation*, but food of some kind *must* be provided in a family, at least when there are children too young to fix it for themselves.

In my mother's generation, Dad supported the family, maintained the car and yard, and took out the trash.

Mom was responsible for the kids and the home.

Nowadays there's no "typical" household. There may be no Dad on site. Mom may go to work, too. Even if she doesn't go to an outside job, she operates in an altogether different world. Neighborhoods aren't safe and full of built-in playmates. Financially strapped schools are relying more on volunteers. Mom may also be looking after her parents or her husband's parents or both.

In short, today's Mom has more responsibilities than our

mothers ever imagined possible. It's not that men are irresponsible; they're just responsible for an arena that hasn't grown as much as ours.

I love it when, in response to these circumstances, someone says, *Oh, that's easy. Just explain to your husband or children that they've got to help out more.* There is certainly something to be said for this (and I'll get to that later), but a division of labor as old as time will not be reinvented in a generation.

In the meantime, we need to look elsewhere, and I suggest it be within.

In one of my early graduate classes, we were asked to read both *Gone With the Wind* and a contemporary book with a woman in constant agony about her role. Our conclusion was that Scarlett O'Hara was "more together" because she had absolutely no doubt in her mind about who she was and who she needed to be.

Women's roles feel like hemlines to me. We used to obey clear fashion trends, which changed with the wind, about the length of our skirts. Even if they didn't work for us, we didn't have to worry about being "wrong" because there was a clear fashion consensus about what was "right." Now, we mostly choose lengths that suit us, but we can be "wrong" if we don't know what's "right" for ourselves.

Clear social consensus about women's roles has also disappeared, with much the same result. In its absence, inner clarity is more necessary than ever before.

We seek clarity about our roles by asking . . .

> *Does this role reflect something I value?*
> *Which of my many roles tugs most powerfully on my heart?*

Understanding whether our roles spring from heartsongs or from something less central is important because our roles beget our responsibilities. People who don't own pets aren't the ones out walking the dogs. Workers outside the health care and emergency fields aren't the ones routinely fielding phone calls in the middle of the night. Not many nonmothers are found baking cookies for the school carnival. If we feel overwhelmed by responsibilities, chances are we are playing too many roles.

As we struggle to keep up, we need to remember that all roles are not created equal. If we try to respond to each with equal intensity, we are destined to feel overwhelmed because there's just not enough of us to go around.

To ease the stress and near-panic that result from too many roles, some of them need to go to the end of the line.

This exercise might help.

Here's a partial list of my own roles in alphabetical order:

CHAUFFEUR

DAUGHTER (AND DAUGHTER-IN-LAW)

EMPLOYER

FRIEND

HOUSEKEEPER

MOM

NURSE

PET-TENDER

PSYCHOLOGIST

SISTER (AND SISTER-IN-LAW)

SPEAKER

VOLUNTEER

WIFE

If I put my list in the order of what requires the most from me, these all show up somewhere in the top five:

CHAUFFEUR
EMPLOYER
HOUSEKEEPER
PSYCHOLOGIST
SPEAKER

If I list the five roles closest to my heart in alphabetical order, the list looks something like this:

DAUGHTER (AND DAUGHTER-IN-LAW)
FRIEND
MOM
SISTER (AND SISTER-IN-LAW)
WIFE

The mismatch between where I give of myself and what I value gives me an idea of priorities I may want to reexamine.

Construct your own lists, starting with the easy alphabetical list and moving on to the tough priority list. If assigning priorities is puzzling, ask yourself . . .

> *Which roles are critical?*
> *Which are not critical but still a priority?*
> *Which are nice but optional?*
> *And which could we lose without ever really*
> *noticing?*

Once we are clear about the roles that are central, we need to be bold about what those discoveries mean.

When my friend Liz decided to go back to school to earn her master's degree, she added a new role and a new layer of responsibilities. These required her to be brutal with her priorities, and friends went to the end of the line. She vanished for two years. It was a hard choice for her and it was hard on her friends, but she recognized it was necessary because she could not maintain the same level of involvement with her friends while adding a major new role.

There are times in life, perhaps many times, when it seems there is nothing we can cross off our lists.

For example, when an aging parent suddenly needs care, few of us feel we can simply ignore our role as daughter. If our list has already been cut to the bone and we are still overwhelmed, the addition of yet another role and its trail dust of responsibilities feels suffocating.

At times like this, we need to be generous with ourselves. We may have to acknowledge that there are people we care about who are going to suffer, probably not forever but for a time; we can hope they will understand.

Just as it is liberating to respond to an expectation with the words *I don't <u>have</u> to do this,* it may be necessary to confront a responsibility with the admission *I <u>can't</u> do this,* not at this price, not today.

Don't expect anyone to applaud your newly arranged priorities, especially if it's someone who stands to lose out. Just because others aren't thrilled doesn't mean you have made a wrong turn; it simply proves that you are traveling without useful signposts.

That's why inner clarity is so important. Listening to our hearts gives us a sense of direction even when the road is not well marked.

> *Life comes in clusters, clusters of solitude, then clus-*
> *ters when there is hardly time to breathe.*

～⌒ MAY SARTON
American writer

# RITUAL

Few women are candid with one another about the responsibilities they let slide. One of the places you can look for strength to reject roles and their trail of responsibilities that are not central to you is in the example of women who have already passed that way.

When you find a woman who seems to be living a balanced life in spite of her multiple roles, ask how she manages that accomplishment. When you find the courage to reject a role whose meaning does not merit the responsibilities it creates, tell other women about your choice.

Every woman who confesses to giving up a responsibility passes permission to another woman to let go of one of her own.

PLEADING
NOT
GUILTY

Shortly after the birth of my second son, John, I plunged into a relentless career that brought me great satisfaction but also bouts of longing and guilt over my daily absence from home. When my youngest son, Michael, was born a few years later, a very brief maternity leave that forced me back to work shortly after his birth only intensified the conflict I felt between my job and motherhood.

Some months afterward, wanting to make up for a bit of what I was certain we were all missing, I took a day off and resolved to be the mom I couldn't be on all the other days. I started off by walking my six-year-old to school, a rare event that made me feel especially motherly.

We swung along for a stretch, enveloped in my maternal satisfaction, until John asked, "Why are you walking with me to school?"

"It makes me feel bad that I work so much and don't get to

spend as much time with you as I'd like," I said, trying to condense my tangle of adult emotions into six-year-old terms. "I miss being with you."

"Oh," he responded with the nonchalance that only true innocence imparts. "I haven't really noticed. I'm in school all day."

I wish I could say that the blazing insight of this revelation obliterated my maternal guilt. It didn't. In fact, I immediately transferred my worries to the baby.

Aha! I said to myself. *Wrong victim! It's Michael I should be worrying about.*

I'm afraid guilt is inevitable when we reject expectations or roles and their trail of responsibilities.

Saying *Yes* to one choice typically requires saying *No* to another. When we say *No* to a choice, we feel we've let somebody down, and women who are raised to be pleasing, serving, and accommodating tend to feel *awful* when they let anyone down.

We tend to feel *guilty*.

I said *Yes* to a job that required me to say *No* to being with my son during the day. Because I thought he expected me to be with him (because somewhere deep inside, I expected to be with him myself) and my choice prevented me from doing so, I experienced a constant, gnawing, fierce, relentless guilt.

Indeed, I was so determined to feel guilty that, when John exposed the error of directing my guilt toward him, I transferred it to Michael without a moment's delay.

Guilt has its uses. Society relies on guilt just as it relies on those expectations that keep us on the right side of the road. It's part of what encourages us to behave in a civilized manner. One of the characteristics of a sociopath is that the person feels no guilt, a deficiency that allows the sociopath to commit criminal acts with no remorse.

But most of the guilt that follows us around like Eeyore's little dark cloud in the Winnie the Pooh story is useless. In fact, guilt is one of the reasons we end up overscheduled and overwhelmed: Our drive to avoid it is so ferocious that we'll say *Yes* to almost anything in order to escape its grip.

A life without guilt is unrealistic. A life immersed in guilt is unbearable. On the path to a simpler life, we need to recognize that some guilt is inevitable, even desirable. We have to honor our genuine desire to be part of a community and guilt's role in that desire.

But we need to stop overdoing it.

Women voice more guilt than men.

In part, this goes back to those roles we just talked about. All of us—men and women alike—tend to feel guilty when we don't perform our "jobs," whatever those may be. The men I see in therapy when they are out of work often experience terrible guilt because they feel they aren't doing their "job" of being a good provider.

But most men today have significantly fewer "jobs" than women. Maybe it's a bit facetious to say that men's jobs are earning a living, taking out the trash, and keeping up the lawn, but only a little bit. Men may be "helping" more with the children and the house and the car pool and the kin-keeping, but "helping" isn't the same as being where the buck stops.

What's more, many women's jobs are performed in emotional minefields. Motherhood is perhaps the biggest one, but there are others, such as daughterhood. When our inability or unwillingness or simple failure to perform a job takes place in one of these zones, that guilt simply can't be matched by the remorse that goes with forgetting to get the garbage on the curb for the trash truck.

Frankly, I think we're a little overavailable for guilt.

I witnessed this when an associate and I left town for a two-day business trip that included her car-pool day. Her husband, who has a flexible schedule, managed to get the kids to school on time but then forgot to pick them up after school. Not until another parent called did Don remember that he was supposed to bring the children home, too.

When my colleague asked her husband what he felt, he listed embarrassment and annoyance with himself. *Imagine!* She felt guilty even though she had done everything possible to make sure the car-pool duties were covered; *I* even felt a wave of guilt sweep over me because we had been together at the time. All Don felt was chagrin.

If our inner lives are to achieve some balance, we need to stop indulging in so much recreational guilt. When we've violated something important, guilt is appropriate. That's how our character sends signals to the other parts of our selves so that we make responsible choices.

As for the other trespasses, the guilt that springs from our failure to fulfill questionable expectations and roles, maybe it's time to broaden our emotional repertoires.

I'd like us to find ways to give ourselves more credit for the "shoulds" that we fulfill and less grief for the ones we miss. We can begin by sifting through our expectations and roles and honestly assessing whether our answers to questions like *Why am I doing this?* and *Is this important to me?* are consistent with our behavior. It is not possible to eradicate guilt, but we can reduce it to more livable levels if we make clean choices that grow naturally from what matters to us instead of contaminated ones that respond to some other hidden agenda.

My close friend Roz and I exchanged Christmas and Hanukkah gifts for years, not just with each other but with all the members of our respective families. When her children hit their teens, I had no clue what to buy for them, and I realized I was dreading those purchases.

Instead of continuing to buy gifts for the whole family, I called Roz and said, "You're the one I care about. You're the one I want to buy gifts for." She seemed relieved. We changed our ritual, buying only for one another.

If I had continued our old custom just to avoid the guilt of possibly disappointing or angering Roz, I would have made a contaminated choice. Because rewriting our tradition was a clean choice, I experienced peace, even though making and acting on the choice was difficult to do.

A simpler life is one where peace rules more often than turbulence. The everyday guilt that is with us like Eeyore's dark cloud is often a symptom of internal conflict. As we sort out our expectations and roles and reconcile them with our values and priorities, we ease inner conflict and begin to emerge from the guilt fog.

> *Women are their own worst enemies. And guilt is the*
> *main weapon of self-torture.*

> ERICA JONG
> *Fear of Flying*

BEWARE
OF THE
DOG

As we make our way down the road to a simpler life, we can count on running into some roadblocks. Chances are, they won't announce themselves with bright, flashing hazard lights; more likely, they will be unleashed dogs that sneak up on us and bark, doing no real damage but scaring us off the path all the same.

These are our histories—our fears, insecurities, misconceptions, and habits, all the sentries beyond which every thought and action pass. There's nothing wrong with them; it's just that, since they follow us everywhere, we can count on them occasionally getting underfoot. And they do represent a danger: If they rev up our anxieties sufficiently, they may deter us from continuing on the path to our simpler lives.

If, as you turn these pages, you find yourself frozen in place, stuck in midjourney, one of these barking dogs may be the culprit. They can show up anywhere and they won't necessarily show up everywhere, but you have reason to suspect the presence of at least one if a suggestion sounds hopelessly intimidating. When that happens, turn back to this chapter to see if you recognize something from your own personal history that is getting in your way.

🐞 LOW SELF-APPROVAL

A lack of self-confidence complicates our efforts to simplify because it contaminates our ability to recognize a good choice and act on it when we find one. Decisions feel bad when they're good because we aren't sure of our own judgment. Choices that are not popular feel awful because they cost us the external approval we count on in the absence of our own.

🐞 A NEED FOR CONTROL

Many of our steps toward a simpler life require exploring new directions and abandoning old ones. Such change always tends to make life seem less under control. If our ability to feel safe and comfortable depends upon exercising a large measure of control over ourselves and our surroundings, simplifying becomes more challenging.

🐞 FAULTY ASSUMPTIONS

If we have bought into the myth that doing the *right* thing will make life easy, the road to simplicity is going to feel like hostile territory.

Simplifying life isn't easy. It requires searching our souls, which can be painful, and changing our priorities, which can be difficult. If we are working on the assumption that if it is *right,* it ought to be easy, these tasks will be unimaginable.

❧ Fear of appearing selfish

We can't simplify our lives without at times putting ourselves before others. When the steps we need to take toward simplicity
seem inconceivable, we may need to examine whether we have
surrendered to the idea that we are selfish if we don't place our
own welfare below that of those around us.

❧ Rampant internal resistance

Just because we say we want simpler lives doesn't mean we
won't find excuses to avoid making them simpler. Whenever we
are asked to look at ourselves and our lives in a new light and to
make choices and take actions based on a different perspective,
resistance is natural. If our resistance is so strong that we can't
move forward, it may be worthwhile to concentrate on simplifying an element of life that doesn't arouse such fierce inner oppo-
sition.

❧ The perfection trap

Perfection has been called the greatest flirt of all. One thing is
sure: It's a mighty obstacle to simplifying life. Simplifying our
lives requires us to let go of all sorts of things. When we let go,
things may appear even more imperfect than they already are. If
we're driven by a demand for perfection, this will feel uncomfortable.

On the western approach to Denver from the Rockies,
there's one sign that always gets my attention. TRUCKERS DON'T
BE FOOLED! it warns. FOUR MORE MILES OF STEEP GRADES AND
SHARP CURVES.

That's what BEWARE OF THE DOG signs are saying. Don't be
fooled.

Just because a suggestion seems impossible doesn't mean that it is. It may mean that something else is at work, something as invisible as gravity—and just as real.

Discovering a barking dog in your path is not cause to abandon your journey. Perhaps you have found an area to work on independent of your search for simplicity—by reading, reflecting, seeking out support from others, even consulting with a professional.

In the meantime, one of the most effective tricks for keeping these mutts at bay is to call them by name.

Think of the neighbor's dog who sets up a menacing racket . . . until you greet him by name. In cases, merely naming these mongrels will reduce their ferocity.

If you find yourself objecting to a suggestion with a severity that seems out of proportion, try to look beyond your immediate response and find its source. If you can say, *This seems impossible because I'm afraid it will make me look selfish,* or, *I think my perfectionism is at work,* that acknowledgment may equip you to face down the influence of your own history.

At other times, we simply need to remember that many watchdogs are more bark than bite. They make our travel more difficult, but they are not impassible. Most barking dogs slink away in the face of calm resolve.

> *You are your past. You are your memories. You can forgive, that's not so hard. . . . But I don't think you can forget all that has made you who you are.*

> BETTYCLARE MOFFATT
> *Soulwork*

III

SIMPLIFYING OUR ORNAMENTAL LIFE

CLOTHING
AS
METAPHOR

Almost nothing in our closets got there by accident. Every garment, on the day we brought it home, served a purpose. Each had something to say . . . about a mood, a fear, a triumph, a role, an expectation, a hope; about something that was real, at least for the moment.

It's as though we've gone shopping for souvenirs.

> *Here's the time I was angry at my husband.*
> *This is when I was celebrating my promotion.*
> *That was the day I felt so intimidated.*
> *There hangs my tenth high school reunion.*
> *This is when I felt broke.*

Women don't need a history of fashion to know that outerwear is a metaphor for what lies beneath the skin. We know it in our bones.

It's behind our tendency as teenagers (when we spend several years with *no* idea of who we are) to dress like everyone around us. It gives us *some* kind of identity in the absence of one of our own.

It explains why, throughout our lives, we call a friend before choosing what to wear in an unfamiliar group. We know all those strangers will size us up by our clothing, and we don't want to send an embarrassing message.

It's why, as adults, our clothes closets tend to be such a jumble. Unless we are exceedingly clear about ourselves or self-disciplined in our shopping, everything we ever were or wanted to be eventually takes shape as something that now hangs between our closets' crowded walls.

In recent years, women have begun to choose clothes according to their personal tastes, traits, and needs rather than according to the dictates of the fashion gods. This has given us wonderful freedom to announce ourselves to the world . . . if only we can figure out what we want to announce.

My friend Cindy Jackson works as a clothing consultant helping clients (mostly women) sort through their existing wardrobes and build new ones. Before she ever opens the closet doors, she sits down with her clients and asks a few questions, including one inquiry that always stops them in their tracks:

> *What do you want people to know about you when
> you walk into a room?*

Who is going to say, *I want them to know I'm a slob?* Nobody I know! We're much more likely to say, *I want people to know I'm friendly* or *fun* or *efficient* or *interesting*.

This is a bonus question. It's a hard one to answer honestly without finding something that we treasure about ourselves. Even if we're stingy with self-praise, the query leads us to an uplifting answer.

I believe that when we dress our bodies in concert with our souls, we instinctively sense the harmony. Whatever their price tag, these garments are the ones that feel like friends when they lie against our skin.

On the other hand, when we're not dressed like the woman we want to announce, when we're "off" a bit, we feel self-conscious and look out of tune.

I once ran into a colleague, a button-down Brooks Brothers sort of woman, at a charity event. When she took off her coat, she unveiled a cascade of taffeta ruffles that she said her husband had picked out for her. Well, it may have announced who her husband wanted her to be, but the woman looked so out of character that I was uncomfortable for her.

If it seems impossible to figure out what suits our selves, it sometimes helps to work backward. What feels great to wear? What prompts people to say, *You look great* (not, *Your clothes look great*)?

Find the common thread that runs through the clothing that feels right and looks right, and we find a piece of ourselves.

There is a place for costumes in our lives.

There are times when we need to dress a part. The jeans and T-shirts I wore to the station for my radio show don't cut it when I make television appearances.

There are times when we just want to have fun. I have a mostly down-to-earth wardrobe because that's the way I see myself, but I also have a couple of things that are just a little seductive. All of us need "play" clothes.

There is room in our closets for our moods. There is room for the seasons. There is room for our many roles. Obviously, lifestyle is a factor. The biggest requirement for a new mother may be clothing that baby spit won't harm. Even geography influences what we choose to wear. Women in New York wear a lot more black than women anywhere else.

Yet when every garment is chosen with the thought, *What do I want people to know about me when I walk into a room?* there will be a consistency regardless of the setting or circumstance. We may be in costume, but we won't be in disguise; our dress will announce us, not camouflage us.

What is appropriate for us will change as our circumstances change.

I know an English teacher who, for a time in the '70s, bought into the idea that students should be "getting in touch with themselves" in the classroom. During this period, Patti was Mother Earth in Birkenstocks and gauze. When her teaching convictions shifted and she decided that what students really needed were basic language skills, she showed up for class in loafers and tweeds.

As different as they were, both styles fit when she wore them because both were consistent with what she wanted people to know about her. When what she wanted others to know changed, her clothing naturally changed as well.

Cindy, the clothing consultant, probably never makes a clothing mistake. It's her *job* to get clothes right. It's not my job, so I do make mistakes, and I always will. That's just fine. If I only make mistakes a quarter of the time, I'm way ahead of days gone by when I made them half the time. My goal is simplicity, not per-fection.

Besides, my clothing mistakes give me something to laugh about. I once discovered that I had eight white blouses hanging in my closet. I had absolutely no need for eight white blouses, but I knew when I bought them that they were safe, and I think I'm a lazy shopper. I kept buying them because I figured, *How can I go wrong with a white blouse?* Too many white blouses, it turned out, was how I could go wrong.

I can now look back on that revelation and laugh, but I still feel a tug when I walk past a rack of white blouses. Recognizing what we want people to know from the way we dress is one thing to achieve in the isolation of our own homes. Hanging onto it when we hit the stores is something else altogether.

If we are to succeed in bringing our selves into tune, we have to learn how to hold the melody in a crowd.

> *Why not be oneself? That is the whole secret of a suc-cessful appearance. If one is a greyhound, why try to look like a Pekinese?*
>
> DAME EDITH SITWELL
> English actress

IF I CAN
ZIP IT,
I BUY IT

So let's watch ourselves shop.

When women opt to shop (not when they *have* to shop), they say that they do it for sport. It's rather like men channel-surfing—we cruise along just to see what's available, pop in and out of the places that seem enticing, and occasionally linger when something really grabs us.

Critics may complain that we have been corrupted by consumerism, they may call us frivolous, but the fact is that women have been the gatherers from earliest times, just as men have been hunters. When we hit the mall, we are playing a part that was established long before any of us individually walked onto the stage.

I'm of the opinion that shopping—you'll notice I didn't say buying—is a fine form of recreation.

In fact, as we have gotten busier, shopping has become one

of the most accessible pleasures left to women. We don't need to plan ahead or make an appointment. We can fit it into whatever time we have—an extended lunch hour if we've got it, twenty minutes if we don't. We can enjoy the comfort of being surrounded by other people with the blissful knowledge that, for these few minutes or hours, we don't have to do anything for any of them. We can eat something we wouldn't normally allow at home (a See's Bordeaux comes to mind, but the possibilities are endless). And as long as we don't buy, it doesn't cost us a cent.

Whether we go designer or discount, or even browse a mail-order catalog, isn't the point. Shopping offers us satisfactions that have nothing to do with what we buy.

We do it with a buddy for companionship.

We go alone to get some time to ourselves.

If we're looking for a little diversion, we amuse ourselves.

If we are in pursuit of something in particular, we do it for the challenge of the hunt.

We gather information about what people are wearing, reading, doing.

When we do it without pressure, shopping gives us the same sense of satisfaction that we might have gotten from a long hot bubble bath with a good book—if only we could enjoy such pleasures without interruption.

As we seek to bring our inner and outer worlds into harmony, our shopping habits are worth considering. The reasons that we shop and the way that we shop are informative beyond what we buy.

For those who indulge in recreational shopping, every expedition tells us something about our needs, our hopes, our insecurities.

That's why it's not what we bring home from these outings

that causes discord and introduces clutter. It's what we take with us that gets us into trouble. Let's examine what we carry along.

If shopping isn't an expression of eternal hope, I don't know

what is.

Every time we walk into a store or hold up a garment for consideration, we brush up against a wish—to be younger/older, taller/shorter, thinner/heavier, or any multitude of alternatives to what we actually are. New clothes can't change the realities, but we live in perpetual hope that they'll create a pretty convincing illusion.

If we are going to fill our closets with clothes that match our spirits, we have to look at these hopes before we ever go shopping. We need to hold them up to what we know about ourselves and say, *Clearer or fuzzier?*

We have to be honest, even brutal, about the hopes that are pathways to ourselves and the ones that are incompatible or out-of-date or, frankly, belong to someone else. And we need to leave the ones that don't fit at home.

When we take unexamined hopes shopping with us, it's like trying on clothes with the lights off: We can't see ourselves clearly, so we are vulnerable to poor choices.

I can remember a time when I was between jobs and feeling unsure of myself. I needed something to wear to an important event, and I wanted an outfit that would fix the inadequacy I was feeling. So I walked into one of those elegant department stores where the clerks dress better than the customers.

I couldn't afford what the clerk pushed on me, but I bought it anyway. I walked out with a dress I didn't love and ended up returning it (after first making sure the clerk who sold it to me would not be there). I spent a lot of time and energy I could have saved if I had caught onto myself *before* I went shopping.

Body image is another hope that gets us into shopping trouble. That's why the clothing manufacturers have started cutting sizes larger. They know we're more likely to buy a smaller size number than a larger size number, regardless of anything else a garment has going for it. *If I can zip it, I buy it.*

Our unexamined hopes trick us into making inappropriate purchases; our appetite for a good deal hoodwinks us into making too many purchases.

We all live in hope that we can look like a million dollars at 70 percent off. When we see a markdown, we make two faulty assumptions: first, that it's okay if we're not thrilled because we're paying half price; and second, that we can buy more because we're spending less on each item. The flaw in the logic is that we rarely feel better about a clothing purchase than we do in the store, so we end up with closets full of disappointments.

My own personal rule is *If I loved it at full price but couldn't afford it, it's a deal on sale. If I wouldn't have liked it much before the markdown, it's not a bargain.*

Besides our hopes, we take our fears shopping with us.

Women's clothing store owners and clerks talk about women who shop from loneliness.

These are the customers who engage the sales associates in long and earnest conversations about what is right for them, possibly even soliciting opinions from other shoppers. Then they buy what appeals to the greatest number of observers without knowing how it really looks or feels to themselves.

We may shop out of desperation or out of anger. Many women say that when they're angry with their husbands, they feel a sense of entitlement that leads them to make their most extravagant purchases.

Similarly, when we are most anxious about money and don't have much to spend, we sometimes make purchases in hope that spending money will subdue our fears about not having any. *If I spend it, it will come* is what I call this philosophy.

Shopping is free, but buying takes time and costs money, and whatever we acquire requires space in our lives and our homes. Few of us have a surplus of these commodities to waste on mistakes, and nobody needs the self-reproach in which they come wrapped.

Understanding what we hope to accomplish in our shopping expeditions gives us a sharper eye and helps us make choices more consistent with the women we are.

> *The great department store . . . derives from the religion of the body, of beauty, of flirtation and of fashion. [Women] go there to pass the time as they would in a church: an occupation, a place where they become excited, where they struggle with their passion for clothes and their husband's budget, and finally with the whole drama of existence, the above and beyond of beauty.*

> EMILE ZOLA
> *The Ladies' Paradise* (1862)

 RITUAL

Gathering may be instinctive, but gathering wisely is a skill that we don't all learn at the same stage or pace. Here are places to begin.

FIND A FRIEND WHO ALWAYS DRESSES AS HERSELF. SHE MAY BE ABLE TO SHOW YOU HOW TO DRESS AS THE WOMAN YOU ARE.

FIND A STORE KNOWN FOR HONEST, GOOD-HEARTED SALES CLERKS.

FIND A SUPER CLERK AND STICK WITH HER ON RETURN VISITS.

FIND A STORE THAT OFFERS THE SERVICES OF A SKILLED PERSONAL SHOPPER AT NO CHARGE.

FIND MAIL-ORDER CATALOGS THAT ALWAYS SATISFY YOU.

FIND THE BRANDS AND LINES THAT WORK FOR YOU.

SHOP WITH THE LIGHTS ON.

LIBERATING
THE
CLOSET

After we've settled on an image that's in tune, we reach the most liberating moment of all: cleaning out the closet!

If we were men, this would be easier. We would just decide how many white shirts we want, how many blue and how many pin-striped, and then thin out our collections of black shoes, brown shoes, and athletic shoes. We would make a pass through the suit collection, toss the socks with holes, consider which sweatshirts were finally too scuzzy for public viewing, and that would be it. Granted, some men are as avid in their collection of clothes as most women, but they are in a distinct minority.

Costuming and shopping are uniquely female pursuits, and the proof is the share of space we take up in our family closets. For us, closet cleaning is not such an easy task; our closets are a veritable riot of styles, sizes, colors, lengths, and functions.

I think of closet cleaning as a ceremony, almost a purifying ritual. At least once a year, I try to block out three hours and pull out everything I own from the closet: clothes, shoes, sweaters. One by one, I take each garment, hold it up in front of me at a full-length mirror, and ask . . .

Do I love it?

If the answer is *Yes,* this is probably a piece that felt "right" in the dressing room and just as "right" when I got home. I wear it a lot and love it now as much as ever. This goes into my first stack.

If I don't love the item, I ask myself: *Do I hate it?* This is the next easiest stack. If I hate it, can't remember why I bought it, feel frumpy when I wear it, then I know it needs a new home. Now I have two stacks.

My third stack is the most dear. These are the sentimental favorites—the dress I chose for my first date with my husband, the nightgown I wore the night I gave birth to my son. These, too, come out of the closet.

Unfortunately, these three stacks barely clear a gap on the rod because, more often when I hold an item up, I conclude that I neither love it nor hate it. These are the pieces that haunt me, and they are legion: garments that are okay, not great, but that get me out the front door in the morning.

Maybe they were bargains I bought because they were too good a deal to pass up. Perhaps they were splurges I've hung onto because they cost so much. Some are stars past their primes, former greats that I've loved nearly to death. Others are reflections of some *me* that I've long since abandoned.

Many of them don't even fit but still take up space as expressions of my hope for return to a previous, more svelte me, or as hedges against reverting to a larger one.

Every garment we own expresses a yearning, no matter how futile or fleeting. The deeper the yearning, the harder it is to part with its symbol. How can we possibly surrender any of them?

Yet garments that don't reflect us need to be bidden farewell. A wardrobe that's out of control makes our lives feel out of control. Clothes that don't fit make us feel bad about our bodies. Clothes that are tired make us feel frayed.

Liberate the closet and we begin to liberate ourselves from all of our false hopes, bad choices, and confusing images.

So now I have my fourth and largest stack, the so-so's. It towers over my little "love-it" pile, but that's okay because simplifying the closet, like simplifying the rest of our lives, takes time. What we're doing every time we go through the closet is training the eye to distinguish what reveals us from what disguises us. Merely recognizing an article as being off-key, even if we can't yet part with it, shows progress.

Of course, parting with our disguises is the point of this exercise. Our rejects need another home—the sooner, the better, even if it's just a closet we never open. Once we no longer have to face them each morning, we can dress ourselves with more confidence and shop for ourselves with more wisdom.

Here is my five-step closet-cleansing ceremony:

STEP 1. IDENTIFY THE NEW HOMES WHERE THE REJECTS WILL GO.

Some women like to consign their clothes, others hold a garage sale. Many donate them to a favorite charity. Pick a destination. No matter how badly they need to go, parting with our clothes is a bit like giving away the kittens we didn't expect the cat to present us: We feel better if we know they're going to a good home.

STEP 2. CALL THE TRUCK, MAKE THE APPOINTMENT AT THE CONSIGNMENT STORE, ADVERTISE THE GARAGE SALE.

Whatever the action, setting the wheels in motion ahead of time encourages us to follow through.

STEP 3. GATHER THE BAGS OR BOXES THAT WILL HOLD THE CASTOFFS.

Clothing left in piles on the bedroom floor has a way of sneaking back into our closets. Bag it or box it, immediately.

STEP 4. REORGANIZE.

Bag up the hate-it stack. Rehang the love-it stack. Tuck the sentimental favorites in a separate, special place where they can be cherished without being seen every day.

Then tackle the so-so's. At worst, rehang them with the love-its and don't obsess about it. They won't hang around for long because, once they're labeled a misfit, their incongruity winks like a neon light every time the closet door opens. Six months from now, they'll look even less at home and may be easier to discard during the next closet ceremony.

A better option is consigning the in-betweens to a space we don't see every day—a spare closet, the basement, a wardrobe box purchased from a moving company and parked in the garage. Again, six months may provide the distance we need to part with these offenders in peace.

The best solution? If courage allows, bag the so-so's with the hate-its and be done with them.

Finally, get rid of the empty hangers, especially the warped metal ones. They are a temptation to refill what we have worked so hard to empty.

STEP 5. SAY GOOD-BYE.

Put the bags on the front porch or drive them away. Tell the friend who collects clothing for the women's shelter that the donations are ready for pickup. I call my friend Kate, who comes immediately to spare me a case of weeder's remorse, a syndrome that sends us fishing through the discard bags in order to give some sad, rejected garment just one more chance. I've even known husbands and children to retrieve articles and shove them back in the closet.

Rarely is this productive. It's hard to miss what wasn't right in the first place.

> *To a woman, the consciousness of being well-dressed gives a sense of tranquility which religion fails to bestow.*
>
> HELEN OLCOTT BELL
> 19th-century American writer

# CELEBRATION

When you have completed your closet cleansing, close the ceremony with a celebration of your triumph.

Brew a cup of tea, allow yourself a break to read something for fun, call a friend for a long, newsy chat.

Or just sit in front of the open closet doors and revel in your accomplishment.

You have earned this moment.

TREASURES ON EARTH

In her small and wise meditation, *Soulwork*, author and teacher Bettyclare Moffatt tells a story about moving into a large, older house filled with windows and doors that look out on a quiet tree-lined street.

For a time, her friends harass her to carpet the bare wooden floors, cover the yawning windows, tame the runaway flower beds, or better yet, just move to a condo that would be more manageable for a single woman.

To every admonition, she politely says *No*. At last, she recounts . . .

> *My friends are finally silent. Until one ventures,*
> *"Well, the house looks just like you."*
> *"Thank you," I respond. "It is."*

If our clothing is a metaphor for our lives, our homes are the metaphor enlarged into a billboard. Our closets contain the tastes and whims and mistakes of just one person who is clothing one body; our houses offer us several whole rooms to fill with the personalities of as many people as our households number. The possibilities are unlimited.

That's why my discussion of our ornamental selves ends with our earthly treasures instead of starting with them. With a little determination, most of us stand a fighting chance to get the best of a five-foot clothes closet. But *the basement! the kitchen! the family room!* One frightening prospect after another.

The prospect of weeding our closets is intimidating; the idea of thinning out the contents of an entire house is almost unimaginable. Yet if we feel relief every time we open a closet containing only what we need and love, how much more soothed we would feel coming home to a house that gave us more than it demanded.

There is a life cycle to our gathering habits.

As very young children, our possessions consist exclusively of what others give to us. Later on, we become collectors. It really doesn't matter what we collect (as the pockets and drawers of any youngster prove). We just need to possess *something* all our own.

By the time we grow up and leave our parents' homes, baseball cards and Barbies have long since lost their allure, although we may box them up and beg our parents not to throw them away. Most of us leave home a little on the bare side.

So we find a job and a roof, and we start to feather our own little nests.

Just how much we acquire depends on many circum-stances, including our incomes, our lifestyles, and our tastes, but just about all of us end up with a lot of what comedian George Carlin calls "stuff" (not to be confused with what other people acquire, Carlin says; that's "junk").

Demographers say that most of us hit our buying stride in our thirties, the decade when our incomes, our families, and our housing are most likely to be growing. After that, we don't con-sume with quite the same appetite, but most of us do go on ac-quiring at a fairly steady clip.

Then, one day, at or somewhere around the curve from midlife, we wake up and look around ourselves. We notice the kids have moved out, we discover restless yearnings, and we ask ourselves, *What in the world am I doing with all this stuff?*

At which point the second stage of our acquisitive life cycle begins: We start shedding possessions.

It's a shame it takes us so long to get around to scrutinizing our stuff. It turns out this is something that matters all along.

Quantity matters. A cluttered home, just like a cluttered closet, makes our lives feel cluttered, and I'm not talking here about tidiness. Clutter is the presence of so much "stuff" that it's hard to see what's there.

Overabundance is a time-waster because we can't quickly lay our hands on items we need. It's a money-waster, too. I now own three flour sifters because every time I needed one, I had to buy a new one because I couldn't find the one I bought for my last sifted recipe.

More than the practical problems, overabundance hides the treasures that actually bring us delight. I know an interior designer who walks through the homes of clients and removes accessories from the tables and shelves.

"If you have too many, you can't enjoy any of them," she explains.

What makes it hard for us to part with our earthly treasures is their meaning.

Like our clothes, our possessions reflect everything we've ever been or hoped to become. Bread-makers and pasta machines, treadmills and exercise bicycles, home computers and electronic phone books. When we look at these trappings and consider parting with the ones that are more hope than reality, we feel the same ambivalence we experience when we clean our closets.

And these practical objects are the easiest to reconsider. It's one thing to acknowledge that we are never going to make homemade peanut butter and then ditch the peanut butter–maker. It's another thing to pitch Grandma's tea set or the kids' preschool art.

And what about souvenirs from travels and other adventures—jobs, romances, friendships? What about the objects that have no function or even beauty but comfort us with their familiarity? What about all the mementos of seasons we have lived and then moved beyond?

Furniture isn't the worst of our problems, because it's big, and we all have a finite amount of space for big objects in our homes. Who has room for three sofas in the living room? The difficulty is all those innocent little things that enter our homes through a door that only seems to swing one way—*in*.

The clue that our earthly treasures are out of control is when they bring us more grief than joy.

I have a collection of old hatpins in holders that are currently heading in that direction. They were once very important;

I can remember hunting for new "finds" with relish. That was many years ago. Now, wherever I move, the hatpins follow me, taking up space in my already crowded basement. I no longer have the same passion for them, nor a place to display them. Yet there they sit.

If the pleasure and the pain of our possessions are in comfortable balance, then we can pass by our earthly treasures to some other, more troublesome nook of our lives. And if possessions are such a source of anxiety that we can't imagine how to begin, perhaps it is better to start somewhere else first. But if our "stuff" is closing us in and we feel up to the task of letting some of it go, it may be a spot to start weeding.

Please don't tackle the whole house at once! Even the most dedicated weeder is likely to be overwhelmed. Setting smaller, more manageable goals ups our chance of success.

These are some of my other tricks for cutting the job down to size:

STEP 1. PICK A HELPER.

When my four siblings and I helped my parents move to a smaller home, we had no problem at all deciding what to toss. It's easy to be irreverent with someone else's possessions. Enlisting a helper helps, but she has to be the right helper—someone who has both a good eye and a good heart. A sister, a friend, a professional. It doesn't matter as long as she isn't co-owner of the "stuff."

STEP 2. PICK A PLACE TO START.

Because success is motivating, I start where I have the greatest chance of succeeding (which, by the way, is definitely *not* the basement). The more overwhelming the job seems, the smaller the initial goal. A single shelf of a single cupboard may be the place to start if the whole cupboard is a disaster.

STEP 3. PICK A TIME.

Time is a great saboteur. Starting on this project without adequate time to complete it assures failure. I make an appointment with myself for a set amount of time on a specific day to undertake these domestic adventures, and I try to be sure that the amount of time and scope of the project match. Then I protect the appointment.

STEP 4. PICK A STRATEGY.

I actually have several of these.

Sometimes I look at the belongings in the space I have chosen to clean and ask myself, *What would make my heart ache if it weren't there?* Oftentimes, an object has some lingering value but, on closer examination, not enough to justify hanging onto it.

I limit how many objects I can exclude, the way a trial lawyer is limited to how many jurors she can exclude. *Okay, I get ten exclusions,* I'll say to myself. I give myself those ten and then box up the rest.

I try to lose what I don't use. If something I don't use is simply taking up space, I consider it a candidate for recycling. Quite recently, I gave away a crêpe-maker that I had received as a wedding gift in 1975 and used once. So what if it took me twenty years to give it up? At least, I finally did.

I try to stop myself from saving more than I can manage. I was told a long time ago that if I saved just one or two precious keepsakes from each of my children's school years, I would feel okay and it would be easier to keep up with the accumulation. I find that advice to be sound. The same strategy is useful against the uncontrolled reproduction of used gift boxes, pencils, and empty pickle jars.

I guard against becoming a "collector." I have one decorative moose head overseeing my family room. I love it, but that doesn't mean I want ten of them. I'm of the opinion that more than three of anything constitutes a collection, and collections come with strings attached. They grow, and they're hard to part with.

5. PICK A NEW HOME FOR THE CASTOFFS AND SAY GOOD-BYE.

Most of us can't dump our memories into the trash barrel. I have a friend who decided several months ago to part with a dinosaur computer she had purchased at great cost when she first went into business for herself. She's been driving around ever since with the system filling the entire storage area of her station wagon because she can't bear to throw it away, yet she can't figure out what to do with it. Decide where the castoffs are going before starting to clear out, and the odds of success increase.

Whether we are examining our closets, our homes, our desks at work, the inside of our cars, or any of the other corners where earthly goods have a way of accumulating like dust balls, we need to have a discerning eye. Every possession has the capacity for bringing us pleasure, whether it's a labor-saving gadget or a priceless memento. Each one also has the potential for becoming joyless clutter.

We all need tokens of the people and the moments we love. They give life to the spaces we occupy. There's just no space for them all.

> *Even the right plant in the right spot can be weedy if there is too much of it.*

~ BARBARA DAMROSCH
The Garden Primer

CELEBRATION

In my house, at all times, is one empty drawer.

It is my reminder of what I have already accomplished in gaining control over my "stuff" and a cheerful little prompt to remind me of how good it feels to pare down my possessions. It is proof that I can do it.

Sometimes, when my life feels scrambled, I just pull out that drawer and feel comforted.

IV

SIMPLIFYING
OUR
DOMESTIC
LIFE

TIDY HOME, TIDY HEART

This may sound a little crazy, but I love doing laundry.

I like buying the soap. I like hanging the clothes on the line (yes, on the line, even though I live in mile-high Denver and own a clothes dryer).

I don't want to send it out. I don't want to hire it done. I don't even want to teach my kids to do it.

As my life has gotten more complicated, I have hung onto the wash on the line while I have let a thousand other things slide.

And I know why: It's because there is something about doing the laundry that connects me to the rhythm of my home and my family. I don't want to let go of it.

I think most of us have some corner of our household world like my laundry that we hold onto, even if we don't know it. And the reason we may not know it is that we've come to feel profoundly ambivalent about the whole business of keeping our homes.

On the one hand, the Music Man of popular wisdom has come to town, jumped on a park bench, and declared, *Ladies, the days of worrying about your house are over! This is the '90s! Skip it! Lower your standards! Don't worry about the house—nobody does anymore!*

Yet we are not persuaded. We find that when we let things slide, we don't feel freed.

If simplifying our domestic lives was just a matter of turning down the expectations and turning up the speed, we would all have iced this one a long time ago. The fact is, this may be the '90s, but our homes still *matter* to us.

They matter more to some of us than to others, and more at some times of our lives than at others. But home matters to virtually all of us, at least sometimes, in some ways. We cannot ignore the emotional investment we have in our homes.

And because home matters, housekeeping matters. There's just no way around it.

There's a place for lower expectations and economy of motion in our domestic lives, but we can't know where to start lowering and economizing until we figure out why we have those standards and what they mean to us.

Yes, Mom had some influence. Maybe she was a great housekeeper and we dust in her shadow. Or she was a terrible housekeeper and we're fighting her example. The hands of June Cleaver, Donna Reed, and Martha Stewart may even be in there somewhere.

But our struggle with homekeeping (to borrow Martha's phrase) goes beyond what we learned and where we learned it.

In fact, housekeeping produces a level of order that makes it easier to live. It's sort of like keeping oil in the car. We do it because it's a pay-now-or-pay-later proposition. Regardless of our homekeeping standards, spending a half-hour searching for the car keys when it's time to leave for work is not productive.

Beyond the functional issues, we value home because it is more than a vault for our "stuff." In the storm of our daily lives, we need a calm eye, and the space where we live with our loved ones is the obvious choice. It's a standing joke in the remodeling business that besides an architect and a contractor, every couple needs a therapist during any renovation to keep their marriage from falling apart.

The kernel of truth in the gag is that our homes are our sanctuaries; when the sanctuary is in chaos, it's hard to get through the day with a desirable level of balance.

And then there's the rhythm.

The downside of housekeeping is that it's time-consuming and it's endless. The reward is that it connects us with the rhythm of our homes, our families, and ourselves.

Part of the reason I love the laundry is because it runs through the whole of my life. It reconnects me with the barefoot summer vacations of my childhood, when fresh wash snapped on the line in the backyard, and with my round-the-clock college days, when I crammed for finals as the clothes turned in a laundromat dryer. When my sons were in preschool, I could determine almost everything they had done and eaten on a given day just by looking at the stains that came home on their clothes. Laundering those clothes was not just another chore; it was another way of being involved with them.

Homekeeping traditionally marked the rhythm of a family's

weeks and months. Monday was washday, Tuesday was ironing day, Wednesday was mending day. Spring cleaning, summer canning, fall raking. The routines are immortalized in nursery rhymes and long memories. Before changing times broke them, these cycles promoted household order and gave life a predictability that people found comforting.

Perhaps we can regain some of that comfort if we find those household tasks that capture the parts of the rhythm that mean something to us. We are so outspoken about the demands of homekeeping, we may be overlooking the possibility that it offers us an intrinsic reward or two.

Maybe you're thinking I've gone around the bend. Rest assured: Spotless is not the point (unless spotless is *your* point). I'm simply suggesting that we be more thoughtful about what matters to us about homekeeping, even if it contradicts the image of the '90s woman.

I believe we would all love our homes to be comfortable and comforting, to offer us a shelter that makes us feel better for entering rather than worse. We all need havens where we can enjoy our children or our friends or just a quiet cup of coffee without being enslaved by our surroundings.

After we acknowledge that home and homekeeping matter, it helps us to simplify our domestic lives if we go on to ask ourselves . . .

> *On a scale of one to five, how much does this matter?*

Some of us will look around ourselves, survey the stacks of old newspapers, the heaps of dirty clothes, shrug, and say, *A one— this is a place to hang my hat.*

You all can move right along. Let's not try to create a something from a nothing.

If the answer is *A two or three, this bothers me, but . . .* then we are really saying, *It is important within limits.* We need to figure out where those limits are and stop fretting. Women who can put up with anything just as long as the dishes are washed should wash the dishes and forgive themselves for overlooking the rest.

If, however, the answer is *A four or five,* if we simply say, *Yes, this matters,* perhaps it is time to make room for *higher* expectations instead of lower ones.

We need to figure out just what it is that we value. My friend Linda, who knows her heartsongs exceptionally well, says what matters to her is the whiff of Pine-Sol she gets when she opens the front door after work on the day the housekeeper has come. "I get a rush that sometimes lasts for two whole days," she says with a sigh of pure contentment.

When what we're after is an orderly home and we couldn't care less about who orders it, there are probably strategies within almost any budget and schedule to make that ideal more attainable. Women's magazines are full of good ideas to simplify housekeeping, and community colleges even offer courses on it—we have a class in Denver called "Debbi Does Dirt."

If what matters is actually *doing* the tasks, we may have to rearrange priorities to make time for them. And if there's not time for everything we want to do, we need to figure out what we want to do *most.*

What parts of the rhythm can we farm out or ignore without feeling disconnected? What parts do we need to save for ourselves? For me, it's the laundry. For another woman, it might be the dusting, or the ironing, or making beds. Comedian Carol Burnett says people invite her to dinner "not because I cook, but because I like to clean up. I get immediate gratification from Windex."

We each need to find the rhythm that soothes us and celebrate our discovery with a grateful heart.

As we order our domestic lives, it helps if we don't set ourselves up to fail.

If it is absolutely essential to us that the mirrors are without spot, giving this particular job to the ten-year-old (or the husband, for that matter) may not be a good idea.

If we have kids, white carpets and crystal on the tabletops may fall in the same category. I suspect even Heloise can't get grape juice out of a white sofa. Most of us have enough other jobs without creating new ones for ourselves.

If personally cleaning every room of the house matters, then recruiting someone else to do it is probably not a good move. If we've decided that all we really care about is that our homes are uncluttered (or some other single goal), we ought to admit it. We can attack one goal with a vengeance and lower our sights for the rest.

There are times of our lives when homekeeping by our preferred standards just isn't practical. One mother of a two-year-old told me she felt as if she lived in a barn because she had packed up all the trinkets that were at risk. We need to comfort ourselves at these times that *this, too, shall pass.*

There are a million how-to ideas for making our domestic worlds simpler. Seek them out. Once we know the how-come, it's easier to figure out which how-to's are worth learning.

I love a beautiful and tranquil home . . . it has been a necessity for me in my life. My job affords me little privacy, so my home has always been my sanctuary.

~ CHER
   Entertainer

THE PROBLEM
WITH CUISINART
GAZPACHO

There are a few friends whose recipes I cherish. Terry and his gazpacho are among them.

Although you don't have to cook it (gazpacho is a cold soup), you do have to mince (not chop, not dice, but *mince*) about a half-ton of tomatoes, onions, green peppers, and other vegetables to concoct that perfect blend of garden flavors.

It takes time. It takes *lots* of time.

One afternoon, I desperately wanted Terry's soup but didn't have the time, so I whipped out my Cuisinart and reduced a mountain of vegetables into mincemeat in no time flat. *Voilà!* Instant gazpacho. I felt so victorious.

Until I discovered the problem with Cuisinart gazpacho: For reasons beyond my own culinary comprehension, the soup's unique flavor depends on all those little veggies bumping hand-minced corners against one another rather than sloshing around in a more randomly hacked-up state.

In short, Cuisinart gazpacho tastes *terrible*.

Cooking is the area of women's busy lives that provokes the loudest groans. After all, we can learn to live with dirty floors, but we can't live without food, and we need it so often. By sunset, most of us have probably been on the go for ten hours or more, often without a break, and then there it is, looming over us like a sledgehammer: *dinner*.

Forget all those rosy announcements about how much more men are doing around the house; studies show we're still whipping up three-quarters of the meals all by ourselves. So we speed through the drive-through. Hit the deli at the grocery store. Nuke and serve a frozen surprise in the microwave. Settle for a bowl of cereal. We look for shortcuts, and they taste . . . well, maybe not terrible, but not particularly appetizing either.

I am not about to proclaim that a simpler life includes home-cooked four-course meals every night. No way would I suggest anything that I'm not willing to do myself. But I do want to suggest that part of our dissatisfaction with the kitchen is that we've become mealtime mechanics.

We go through whatever motions (the fewer the better) that are absolutely necessary to make sure nobody starves. We settle for convenience foods that don't do much for our bodies, and we entirely overlook the rituals of food that might do something for our souls.

Yet, food—the making of it and the sharing of it—remains the timeless, universal bond of everyday living. In virtually every human society, bread or its equivalent is revered as the staff of life. When we deny its importance, we cut ourselves off from the heart and soul of living.

Maybe we can't return to the times when food was the core of a family's existence. I have yet to hear a woman complain that she missed out because she was born too late to participate in the rituals of planting, cultivating, harvesting, preserving, preparing, and serving practically every bite that hit the family table.

Still, almost all of us express longings for snatches of those rituals—for the house-filling aroma of stewing fruit, for the savor of homegrown tomatoes, for the friendly chaos of cooking in a kitchen full of women. Why else do we have boxes of Mason jars collecting dust in the garage? Or exhaust ourselves putting Thanksgiving dinner on the table? Or spend half our grocery store time in the produce section snapping the green beans and thumping the watermelons?

Perhaps that's why we gripe so much about cooking—because our overscheduled lives have wrung everything out of it but the drudgery, and we know something's missing but we just don't know how to get it back.

As we simplify our lives, what we want is food that replenishes our spirits as well as our bodies.

We have to figure out, as we did with our households, what matters to us about it. Process or product. Taste, variety, cost, or nutritional value. The number of minutes it takes to progress from shopping bag to tabletop, or the number of family members who will eat it without complaint.

Then we have to figure out how to respect what matters about food without driving ourselves crazy in the process.

If necessary, we can work backward. What brings us joy about food?

I'm convinced that cutting corners on the food front is inevitable for all but those women who choose to put food at the very top of their priority lists. I just worry that sometimes we cut out more than the corners. If we can find out what matters to us about food, we can figure out how to cut the corners without cutting the nourishment of the body *or* the spirit.

For example, if making our food is what personally counts, we need to be mindful of visiting too many drive-throughs. We can't avoid cutting that corner sometimes, but we need to find days—no matter how few—when we don't. The satisfaction those days provide sustains us for all the others when we have to simply *make do.*

Sometimes we need to allow ourselves more time. In all fairness, my gazpacho disaster was not entirely the Cuisinart's fault. Part of the soup's charm, it turned out, lay in the ritual of creating it. That's probably why some people persist in making fruitcakes for friends who just throw them away. Feeding the body isn't always the point; sometimes doing things the hard way is necessary to feed the soul.

As for what we put on the table, perhaps it would help if we looked at how we get it there through different lenses than the ones offered to us in the commercials.

Is it really more *convenient* to drive through traffic to the supermarket after work, cruise the aisles for instant dinner, stand in the checkout line, and then struggle through more traffic to get home . . . or to sauté a couple of chicken breasts and toss a salad with ingredients already on hand?

And is it really more *economical* to buy take-out because there are no groceries in the house than to pay the supermarket five dollars (the going rate in Denver) to fill your entire shopping list for a week and have the order waiting for speedy pickup?

Frankly, I think I hear the Music Man again.

Regardless of what finally reaches the table or how it gets there, it matters how we share our food.

I once took a cooking class from chef and author Lynne Rossetto Kasper, who summed up the issue nicely when she asked us, "Can you imagine a coach in Italy scheduling soccer practice during the dinner hour?"

The table is where our families can come together to share our days and ourselves. More than any other single place, it is where our personal culture is passed along, in the kinds of food we eat and the way we eat them, in the topics we discuss and the routines we observe. Even when we eat alone, meal-taking can be a ceremony . . . or a hurried habit.

Most of us, whether we are a single or a multitude, are fighting the current to get to the dinner table. We need to step out of the current as often as we possibly can. There is no better time to turn off the television, turn on the answering machine, turn away the world. It is not just what we eat that matters; it is also the ritual of eating that fosters our sense of wholeness and belonging.

M.F.K. Fisher, the writer who raised American food writing to a literary art, once said, "It seems to me that our three basic needs, for food and security and love, are so mixed and mingled and entwined that we cannot straightly think of one without the others. So it happens that when I write of hunger, I am really writing about love and the hunger for it, and the warmth and the

love of it and the hunger for it . . . and then the warmth and richness and fine reality of hunger satisfied . . . and it is all one."

For these reasons, we must meet over the dinner table.

There is a communion of more than our bodies when
bread is broken and wine is drunk.

M.F.K. FISHER
The Gastronomical Me

 RITUAL

You know all those articles that say meal preparation is more manageable if you plan ahead, shop ahead, and cook ahead? I hate to admit it (because I haven't mastered this myself yet), but they're right.

In her cookbook *Keep It Simple: 30-Minute Meals from Scratch,* Marian Burros offers up several other useful tips for simplifying meal prep without giving in to the fast-food gods.

Among her useful tidbits:

- Keep the cupboard stocked with staples.
- Know where to find them.
- Keep the cooking equipment in good repair.
- Stop worrying about exact measurements (unless you're baking).
- Forget about mincing (so much for gazpacho).
- Give up on stewing and roasting (go for broiling, boiling, sautéing, and simmering).
- Forget about whole meat (whole chickens, whole roasts); stick with pieces.
- Start with the food that takes longest to cook.

"Being busy," promises Burros, "doesn't mean you have to settle for second best."

FALSE ECONOMIES
AND
OTHER LIES

Shortly after first-class postage rates took their latest hike, a reader sent a letter to Abigail Van Buren's syndicated advice column commenting on her reaction to the "outrageous" increase to 32 cents. As an act of protest, the reader had gotten into her car and driven 15 miles to pay her utility bill in person.

"As I was standing in line waiting to pay, I thought about how I had just spent $1.26 for gas and an hour of my time," she wrote. "Next time, I'll just put a 32-cent stamp on it and drop it in the mailbox."

I wish I had a calculator that computed the value of all my own economic strategies just as clearly. The false economy of driving across town to avoid an extra 3 cents for a stamp is easier to see than the bigger, costlier falsehoods that sap the vigor from every single day.

* * *

Sportscaster Phyllis George has said that the most popular labor-saving device is money. Regrettably, she's right. If we just had enough money, we know, we could pay someone to take over a chunk of our to-do lists. It would be almost as good as that TV commercial of a few years ago that showed people whizzing into a drive-through and ordering a few extra minutes; it would be like buying time.

It is also about as far-fetched.

Time . . . it's what study after study comes up with when people are asked what they would like to change about their lives. In part, our hunger for simpler lives is a hunger for the time to address all those unsatisfied longings that tug at our hearts.

Since neither time-dispensing drive-throughs nor piles of money are on the horizon, we can only feed this hunger by finding time in other, more creative ways.

We can start by weighing the claims upon our time as brutally as "Dear Abby's" reader weighed the cost of getting around a higher-priced stamp. Everybody's time is worth something. If we are paid by the hour, we know exactly what our time is worth, at least to an employer.

If we don't work for pay, our time still has value because we spend it providing services of value. I know a couple who bought a large life insurance policy for the wife because they figured out that if something happened to her, the husband wouldn't have enough money to pay for all the services she was providing as a full-time homemaker.

We don't hesitate to question economics when it comes to spending our money. What we need is to be just as zealous about questioning the economics of spending our time.

The husband of a friend thought she should darn his socks, for which he paid about a dollar a pair at a discount warehouse. His mother had darned his socks, and his first wife had darned his socks, so he suggested that my friend should too. After she showed him the cost of darning socks at the hourly rate she charges her consulting clients (to say nothing of the time she needed to learn how to darn in the first place), the discussion ended.

Once we start placing a value on our time, we possess a gold standard for measuring the *real* cost of every activity that engages us—whether it's darning the husband's socks or washing the car or being a community volunteer.

Please! I'm not suggesting that we free up time to work more. What we want is to free up time to refresh our souls. When we discover we're wasting money, it often changes our spending habits. What we're after here is a view of our time that enables us to evaluate *when* we're wasting it. Just as a dollar saved is a dollar earned, an hour saved is an hour gained.

And speaking of dollars saved, ferreting out hidden costs and rerouting the dollars is another way to "find" money with which to "buy" time.

Another friend was going through one of those intense periods at work when there was barely time to breathe, much less to get dinner on the table. Convenience food, drive-throughs, restaurants—*anything* was more feasible than cooking.

Then someone suggested that a struggling college student might be grateful for the opportunity to earn a few dollars a week cooking and freezing multiple meals for the family to eat during the workweek. *Pay someone to cook!* She was horrified. To a woman who still wasn't comfortable with the idea of hiring someone to clean her house, paying to have meals cooked sounded unimaginably extravagant.

Then she sat down and calculated how much it was draining the budget to bring home convenience and fast food every night, and her reaction changed. She called the placement office of the local college and found Laurie, a student delighted with executing three or four recipes that could be refrigerated or frozen. My friend not only saved money but found herself with a few nights a week when she didn't have to worry about cooking *or* rustling up take-out.

We all have habits that would look different if we evaluated them, just as the "Dear Abby" reader looked at her protest of the 32-cent stamp or my friend studied the cost of a "cook." When we go out of our way to save a penny a gallon on gas or drive to three different supermarkets to use all the newspaper coupons, we may or may not save money once we add in the cost of gas, and we certainly don't save any time.

Sometimes we dismiss time-saving ideas that would simplify our days with the words *Oh, I can't afford that.* Perhaps if we would weigh their expense against the true but hidden costs of the alternatives, it would provide us with "found" money that we could use to pay for a little more help.

Since we've been considering the way we approach homekeeping and cooking, it's worth looking at another aspect of false economy: the space it takes.

When I was a divorced young mother in graduate school, my oldest son, Jim, and I lived in the married-student housing on campus in Michigan. Like student housing everywhere, my apartment was cheap and small—about 500 square feet.

Besides all the necessary trappings of daily life, nothing would do for me but a box of Tide laundry detergent about the size of a small television set and a family-size bottle of catsup that took up half a refrigerator shelf. My mother had always bought these economy sizes for our family of seven, so that's what I reached for when I shopped.

In truth, even at that barren time in my life, I was better off scraping up the extra pennies for smaller sizes than trying to find the room for bigger ones.

Buying the economy size or buying in bulk makes sense for those who have room to store these extras. It usually does cut down on costs and shopping trips. But if our savings are squeezing us out of our space, these economies may be false as well.

> *Mere parsimony is not economy. . . . Expense, and great expense, may be an essential part of true economy.*
>
> EDMUND BURKE
> *Letters to a Noble Lord* (1796)

BOOTING UP

While we're trying to sort out the true economies from the false in order to simplify our days, there's a whole new frontier to explore these days: technology.

My friend Earline sums up one of the hazards technology presents to our search for simpler lives.

"When we come home from a trip," she says, "I always go first to the patio to see what has bloomed. My husband goes to the answering machine to see who has called."

Earline has lived long enough and wisely enough to know that the blooms on the patio bring her more pleasure, wonder, and connection with life than anything waiting for her on the answering machine.

Yet how many of us would follow her there?

There is not much doubt that telephones were an improvement over hand-carried messages, but now we also have car phones, cellular phones, and air phones, not to mention call waiting, call forwarding, caller ID, and, of course, the good old-fashioned telephone-answering machine.

There are fax machines in our offices, homes, and cars and e-mail on our computers. And who waits days for a letter to arrive? Now we have overnight delivery.

Technology has seduced us at every turn with its promises of speed, efficiency, convenience, and economy. We buy the promises because we desperately want simpler lives. Too often, we have bought a lie.

We need to remember that almost nothing of what matters to us in life can be captured on a microchip. We have relationships— with ourselves, with others, and with the greater world—that actually suffer in the presence of unlimited technology.

I am reminded of a self-employed woman who used to print out all her work on a letter-quality daisy-wheel printer. It required four minutes to print one page, meaning a four-page document took more than a quarter-hour to print. When her computer was tied up printing, the woman would take those minutes to stretch her legs, go to the kitchen to pour an iced tea, scan the mail, touch bases with her husband, check up on her kids.

Then she bought a laser printer that whipped out a page in a mere eight seconds.

A document that once took her an hour to write and fifteen minutes to print now could be printed in thirty-two seconds. She couldn't even get to the bathroom and back in thirty-two seconds.

Suddenly the tempo of her whole workday picked up.

She had gained speed, efficiency, convenience, and even economy. She had paid for it with her breathing room. Instead of saving time, she had just turned up the speed.

I see the same trap closing around restaurant diners carrying on portable-phone conversations while theoretically eating with someone else, around moviegoers sprinting from the theater to answer a pager's call, around tourists catching the sights through the lens of a camcorder.

In each case and so many others like these, technology has been allowed to insert itself between us and life itself.

These examples, however, do more than demonstrate the problem technology presents; they hint at the solution.

My friend could have hit the "print" button and gone on down to the kitchen as she once did, even though the document would be ready in half a minute. She didn't have to let the speed of her printer dictate the pace of her day. She could have taken advantage of the benefits of the new technology without giving up the advantages of the old.

The idea just didn't occur to her. True to her work-ethic roots, she assumed that if more time became available for work, she should do more work.

Like her, most of us simply accept the idea that if technology makes something possible—to stay in touch with the office while at a meal or a movie, to capture our memories on tape—we have no choice but to exercise the possibility.

This simply isn't true.

In our simpler lives, we want to pick and choose among technology's promises. Technology won't limit itself; we have to set limits for it if we don't want it to come between us and more meaningful parts of our lives.

Consider this: Other than housekeeping and cooking devices, most of the technological wonders that have found their way into our homes in recent years were originally designed for the *workplace,* not for the home. Computers, facsimile machines, multiline telephones, and all the various telephone-related innovations were designed to make *offices and businesses* more efficient. They don't deserve the same position in our homes.

For example, I have mixed feelings about having a fax at home. On one hand, a fax allows me to get things to and from others without leaving my house. On the other hand, I don't want to be available to the whole world while I'm at home.

My solution has been to allow people to fax documents to me without letting them know that they're reaching my home (actually, a remote upstairs closet of my home where the intrusion is further minimized). Sounds silly, but it works.

Now, caller ID is one technogadget that actually does simplify my life. It allows me to know who is calling without picking up the phone or screening the answering machine. This helpful little device enables me to turn off the answering machine altogether (no messages to return!) and still know who has called (in case I can't resist calling back to find out if I missed something important).

This idea of not missing things is another fraud that deserves exposing.

Many communications gadgets that create the relentless sense of urgency consuming us are designed to prevent us from missing any call or caller.

Frankly, a lot of them are actually worth missing.

Junk calls are an obvious example, but there are others. When we can't be reached to answer a question, people often figure out the answer on their own. When someone is looking for a volunteer and our phone isn't answered, the caller moves on down the list. There are even crises in the lives of friends and loved ones that get resolved quite nicely in spite of the fact that we can't be reached by phone, fax, Fed Ex, or e-mail.

Part of what makes our days feel so overrun is the sense that our time and energy are vastly outstripped by the demands made upon them. If technology is a channel funneling demands into our lives, maybe we can reduce the flow by taking greater control of the pipeline.

One of those phrases that seems to come encoded in every mother's vocabulary is *If it's important, it will wait.* My brother Bob puts it another way: *Nothing important is urgent, and nothing urgent is important.*

Technology turns up the sense of urgency in our lives. If we put limits on it, we relieve some of the urgency so that what matters can stand out.

> *The devices are advertised as time-savers, but in reality they devour time. Leisure time, time to be alone, time for thinking is gobbled up in instantaneous communication so you have more time to get more work done.*
>
> ANN SCHRADER
> *Denver Post* staff writer

 RITUAL

Sometimes it takes dispensing with something temporarily to discover that it is dispensable. One of the ways to sort the urgent from the important is to shut down the technology pipeline entirely for a few days. In the silence, we may find it easier to "hear" what really matters.

If you feel overwhelmed by the demands on your time, I suggest taking a week off from any—or all!—of the following. At the end of the week, evaluate what you have missed and what you have gained. If the gains outdistance the misses, you may want to impose permanent limits of how much of the world these devices bring into your personal life:

UNPLUG THE TELEPHONE-ANSWERING MACHINE.
DISABLE CALL WAITING.
IGNORE THE TELEPHONE!
TURN OFF THE CAR OR CELLULAR TELEPHONE.
DISCONNECT THE FAX.
TAKE THE BATTERY OUT OF THE PAGER.
GO OFF-LINE.

To further test the potential benefits of choking off the pipeline, consider turning off some of the information/entertainment technology that has a way of increasing the pulse rate of our days.

GO A WEEK WITHOUT READING THE NEWSPAPER.
TUNE OUT BROADCAST NEWS.
DON'T TURN ON THE TELEVISION.
UNPLUG THE CABLE.
CHECK THE GARDEN FOR NEW BLOOMS.

V

SIMPLIFYING OUR WORK LIFE

PUTTING WORK
IN
ITS PLACE

One of the more curious symptoms of the imbalance of our lives is that we *think* we work more hours than we actually do.

When people are asked to report how many hours they worked in the previous week, social scientists find, respondents *report* working more than they *record* if they keep minute-to-minute diaries of the same workweek.

In 1965, the difference between perception and reality was one hour. By 1985, it was seven hours and presumably growing. The biggest discrepancies were in the self-reports of women.

The experts are still arguing over what all this means, but I have my own theory: Regardless of how many hours we are working, it *feels* as if we're working more than ever before. Our perception has become our reality.

This fuzziness in our vision suggests at least two approaches to simplifying our work lives: We may change the reality, or we may change our perception of the reality. Either approach holds hope for bringing the place of work back into focus.

There is no denying the enormous importance of work, irrespective of our job description or employer.

We all rely on it for financial stability, and the vast majority of us rely on it for emotional rewards. In one Gallup survey of working mothers with children under eighteen, 70 percent said they work in part to feel good about themselves.

Work also matters on a most basic level because we literally spend so many hours doing it. In a full-time job, we spend more waking hours at our workplace and commuting to and from it than we do in our own homes.

Yet if our lives are to be anchored with what matters most to us, work needs to know its place.

Few of us would rank work at the top of the list of what we cherish most deeply. The old saw that nobody ever reached the end of life and concluded, *I wish I had spent more time at work* is rooted in truth.

When we know in our souls that work is not the heart of our lives, yet we live every day as if it were, we begin to hear a hollow ring at our core.

We know we are living around our work rather than working around our lives when decisions that set the pace of our lives routinely accommodate the demands of our jobs, when we make choices like these . . .

> *The boss walks in at 4:30 P.M. with a two-hour project on a workday that is supposed to end at 4:45. We reschedule the evening instead of rescheduling the project.*

The supervisor asks for volunteers for overtime.
Even though our financial survival doesn't hinge
on signing up, we agree to stay late although it
means passing up personal pleasures.

We have a half-hour commute to work each way.
We spend it making business calls on the cellular
phone instead of savoring the drive as an oasis of
solitude in our crowded day.

In more than ten years as a radio psychologist, I talked with hundreds, perhaps thousands, of women who wrestled daily with these dilemmas.

What I learned is that most of us who find ourselves depleted by our work operate on three powerful assumptions that prevent us from bringing it into balance with the rest of our lives.

❧ I HAVE NO POWER OVER MY JOB.

This shows up in our belief that we will jeopardize our job security or status if we try to change our work environment or turn down demands, no matter how unreasonable.

❧ I HAVE NO POWER TO ESCAPE MY JOB.

This assumption makes itself felt in a sense of entrapment—that no matter how bad the job, we are powerless to get out of it.

❧ I HAVE NO POWER OVER MY FEELINGS ABOUT THIS JOB.

This evidences itself in an enormous sense of hopelessness, a conviction that there is absolutely nothing possible that could change how we feel about our work.

The common denominator in all three assumptions is *power*. Someone else has it. We do not.

Putting work in its place and keeping it there requires plugging the holes where it is seeping into the other substantive corners of life. We can accomplish this only when we assume more control over our work lives.

This begins with challenging the three assumptions that enable work to control us and then acting on the information this exercise provides.

We start by asking ourselves . . .

> *How do I know I can't control my work?*

When the boss walks in at 4:30 with that two-hour project, we can test our power by responding . . .

> *I will be happy to stay until five to work on this, but*
> *I have other commitments and will have to finish*
> *the rest in the morning.*

If we are struggling to balance work and home, we can approach the supervisor and suggest . . .

> *I could be more productive if I started work an*
> *hour earlier and left an hour earlier. This would*
> *enable me to get more done during the early quiet*
> *while providing me with flexibility in my life.*

When our workload feels crushing because of unrealistic demands, we can force the boss to share responsibility for the problem and the solution by saying . . .

*I consider it important to complete every
assignment to the best of my ability, but I find
myself with more projects than I can handle well.
Of the assignments I currently have, which five are
the most important to you and in what order?*

109

Those of us who are skilled, and whose skills make us valuable employees, will often be pleasantly surprised to find we can set more limits than has been our habit. It often turns out our employers would rather accommodate us than lose us.

By speaking up for ourselves, we confirm what they knew but perhaps had forgotten: that we are valuable and need to be treated accordingly. When we lean against the boundaries, we feel them give, and we produce real improvements in our work conditions and an improved perception of work.

*To be successful, the first thing to do is fall in love
with your work.*

SISTER MAY LAURETTA

 RITUAL

To begin putting work in its place by reducing its control over your life, try these techniques:

1. REHEARSE.

Preparation builds confidence. When you're ready to test or push the boundaries of your control, practice—in your mind, with your mate, with a friend. Know what you're going to say and get comfortable saying it.

2. ASK.

When I left high school, I went to work as a typist for North American Rockwell. After about three months, I knew I wanted to move on. Looking through a policy manual one day, I found an item about the firm's educational leave program. I told my boss I wanted to take one so I could go to college.

"But that's for engineers," he said.

"That's not what it says here," I replied.

I got the leave, they paid a portion of my tuition, and I had a summer job waiting for me at the end of the school year.

Generally speaking, people who get raises are the people who ask for them, and the same is true of other arrangements that could change the conditions that make work difficult for us.

Ask, and you just might receive.

3. ANNOUNCE.

Head off problems at the pass with an announcement.

If you are tired of being the one who is asked to pull the holiday shift, it's never too early to let the boss know you won't be available. When you tell him in October, *I just wanted to let you know as early as possible that I won't be available to work on Christmas Day,* you are in a position of strength when he walks up to you on December 12 and says, *By the way, I've given you the Christmas shift.*

4. BE UNAVAILABLE.

People who take advantage of our availability are just aiming at the easiest mark. If they don't hit the target with us, they'll move on to somebody else.

5. REMEMBER THAT THE FIRST *No* IS THE HARDEST.

It is absolutely true that nothing succeeds like success. The emotional and practical payoffs of saying *No* and changing a work reality are so immense that it won't be nearly as difficult the next time.

SHIFTING GEARS

Some of us lack job skills or possess skills that are out-of-date or discounted by our employers. When *we* test the limits, the boundaries don't budge, and the attempt confirms our fear that we are without power.

This unhappy finding requires more dramatic steps if we stand a fighting chance of balancing work with the rest of what matters to us.

It requires shifting gears.

Several years ago, I participated in a "Career Day" sponsored by a local college. It involved allowing a student to spend the day tagging along with me at work.

The student who arrived at my door early that morning was not a typical coed. Older than I, she was the married mother of two teenagers, a perfect example of what educators call a "re-entry" student.

It turned out that Sherrie had always dreamed of a career in radio but had married young and started a family quickly. Now that the children were almost out of high school, she had decided to finish her education and pursue her dream.

Her husband wasn't wild about the idea. He foresaw that a college degree and a career would alter *his* life in ways he didn't particularly relish.

He agreed that his wife could go to college upon one condition: They would have to sell their house and move into an apartment. He figured she would never give up her home and the financial security it represented.

Instead, she said, "Fine, let's sell the house."

My "Career Day" student had taken control of her work life in two ways.

First, the prospect of earning a college degree changed her *perception* of her independence.

Second, by acquiring skills that would open up new job opportunities for her, she was in the process of changing her work *reality.*

Shifting gears takes many forms, not all of them as radical or personally costly as Sherrie's. Here are just a few that help.

NEW SKILLS

When we lack control over our work life because we lack skills that would make us valued by an employer, shifting gears probably means getting more training.

When our own employer offers a training or retraining program, this is an excellent place to start. Most employers don't, which makes it likely that retraining will disrupt our lives for some period of time as we add the role of "student" or "trainee" to all the other roles we hold.

As difficult as those disruptions may be, if they pave the way to jobs that liberate our spirits, they represent a long step toward a simpler life.

❦ New spending habits

Let's face it: Most of us aren't working to squirrel away money for a cushy retirement. The national savings rate makes that pretty obvious. We work to earn to spend.

One way we can increase our control over a draining or demoralizing job is to reduce our financial dependence on the job by reducing our spending.

Fortuitously, the very process of simplifying life naturally helps with this challenge because it lowers our cost of living. A life lived close to the heart is just plain cheaper. As we give priority to what matters, we make fewer "compensatory" purchases—like buying toys for the children because we are too busy or too tired to play with them. And if we're only buying what belongs in our lives, the potential universe of fitting acquisitions shrinks.

By reducing our financial requirements, reduced consumption creates work-related choices that otherwise might be out of reach, such as going back to school, changing employers, or changing careers.

❦ New work habits

Any one of these insidious work habits can make us feel married to our jobs. Work and our perception of work are relieved and life is more balanced when we loosen the grip of even one.

- We allow work to follow us everywhere.

  We give free rein to gadgets that make us instantly and universally available, creating a sense that we walk through life wearing an "On Duty" sign.

- We multitask.

  Instead of working the old-fashioned way—one task at a time—we send faxes from the car, bring staff reports to the kids' sporting events, catch up on professional reading while we exercise. We subscribe to the philosophy *If I can do it, I should,* which makes it possible to work every waking moment.

- We regularly work late (or arrive early).

  Keeping long hours leaves no room for other activities that could balance work with the more soulful parts of life. What's more, it generally ends in fatigue and *lower* productivity.

- We routinely take work home.

  This is the at-home version of long hours. It produces the same results.

These habits tend to give our jobs mastery over the rest of our lives. Replacing them with habits that set limits for work puts us back in the driver's seat.

NEW PERCEPTIONS

If perception is reality, changing our perceptions can change our sense of work reality.

When we find ourselves in a seemingly unbearable work situation, we may be able to change our perception of the situation by building an escape route.

Taking a class in the evening, making connections with a

work group in another part of the plant, reducing our credit card balances so that we require less income, are among the many ways we can expand our options.

Knowing an escape route is under construction can be freeing even when we can't use it right away.

Which brings us to the long view. Another escape route involves learning to view intolerable work situations as a means to an end that we never let out of sight . . .

> *I will stay at this job for two more years in order to complete the college fund for my daughter.*

> *I can do this for six months because the coworker who is making my life miserable retires then.*

> *I will put up with this until my needed medical treatment is complete, and then I will leave.*

When we view work as a means of reaching an important goal, it becomes more of a *choice,* less of a *trap.*

On occasion, nothing will do but to change employers or professions.

These are the most wrenching shifts of all. They may involve a reduction in pay, benefits, convenience, or other features. They probably require leaving behind people with whom we have become connected.

Yet if we ask ourselves, *Is this the way I want to live my life?* and answer *No,* it is time to find a way to move on.

No paycheck in the world is big enough to compensate for the hopelessness and despair that result from remaining in a job that sucks the joy out of life.

There's a huge percentage of people out there who never decide what they really want to do with their lives. They'd like to follow their dream, but they just settle for what they do. Then it's too late.

"SOURDOUGH SLIM" CROWDER
The Yodeling Cowboy

HOME SWEET OFFICE?

One of the most seductive work alternatives to emerge for women in recent years is moving our work into our homes. Talk about shifting gears!

No commute, no work wardrobe, no office politics. Simplified child care. No more lying to the boss when the kids are sick or an aging parent needs immediate attention.

When our lives are overwhelming and work is part of what overwhelms us, it is normal for us to fantasize about alternatives. Especially as we read about the glories of home work and perhaps even watch our friends successfully do it, rare is the woman who doesn't at least give home-based work a passing thought.

Letting home do double time as workplace is a liberating, viable alternative for some women, a creative alternative to real problems.

I have a friend who reports on the business world for a national magazine from her suburban New York home. Having postponed motherhood until her forties, she didn't want to spend it in a Manhattan high-rise. Over the last ten years, she has convinced a succession of editors to accommodate her desire to work from home.

She loves her home office. She loves working in tennies, working free of distraction, and working where her son, Josh, can pop in and say hello when he comes home from school.

Yet for other women, the very same picture couldn't be less appealing.

On the opposite coast, Sally is a partner in a two-woman public relations agency. Although she could easily operate from home, she absolutely refuses to give it a try.

"I would never feel like I was at work," she insists.

Moving our work into our homes requires more than listening to the longings of our souls. It also requires studying them in light of our habits, our lifestyles, our families. We need to be knowledgeable and honest about . . .

OUR NEED FOR SOCIAL CONTACT IN OUR WORK.

Social contact is one of the reasons a great number of women work. If we would die on the vine in isolation, home is probably not our ideal workplace.

OUR NEED FOR ORDER IN OUR SURROUNDINGS.

If we haven't gotten a handle on managing our homes, bringing work into them will simply make work feel as disorderly as home already does.

Our need for privacy.

Working from home invites the outside world into our houses and shoves our private worlds into our workplaces. The result is almost inevitably less privacy at home and less privacy at work. If that sounds uncomfortable, working at home is likely to feel uncomfortable.

Our need for structure.

Some of us respond best to structure, like canaries who go to sleep when their cages are covered. We work in our work setting and do nonwork tasks outside of work.

If we can't internally set the limits that a workplace normally provides, working from home becomes a giant step toward a more complicated life. A home workplace is *always there,* waiting to be used. Our inability to draw clear lines between our work time and our private time puts us at risk to work twenty-four hours a day, seven days a week.

Our ability to set limits for others.

Setting limits for ourselves isn't the only challenge of working from home. Women who have tried it say they also have to set limits for their mothers, their friends, the neighbors *(Since you're home anyway, could you let the repairman in?)* and a multitude of others who needed virtually no regulation at all when we left home to go to work.

Our kids.

Children of all ages have a degree of trouble with the concept that *Mom is here, but she's not here,* but it is more problematic for some than for others. In deciding whether to work from home, mothers need to consider the tolerance zone of their work for children and the tolerance level of their children for outside work.

Every mother knows the frustration of carrying on a phone conversation with a friend while her child works on an Academy Award for acting in an attempt to get her attention. When the caller is a key client or a major customer or anyone who thinks you're actually *at work* (which, by definition, does not include the background sound effects of siblings beating the daylights out of each other), our professional effectiveness can be at stake.

If the very thought of working from home makes your chest tighten, this is probably not a simplifying strategy you want to attempt.

If it doesn't, it may be worth a try. For some women, home work not only simplifies the logistics of their jobs but offers the possibility of pursuing a career that brings them benefits that outside jobs didn't offer.

I met Miriam when she worked part-time in a quilt store in Denver. When she decided that she wanted to spend more time with her daughter's family in Grand Junction, she turned her quilting hobby into a home-based business. The sale of her quilts replaced the income provided by her previous outside job, and it gave her a more relaxed lifestyle that meshed with her heartsongs.

One of the home work options that tugs on the hearts of many women is being a full-time homemaker.

We add up the cost of a wardrobe, transportation, and day care and find that work makes little financial sense. Or, it makes financial sense, but it makes no emotional sense. We're in the 30 percent of working mothers who don't feel better about ourselves because we work outside our homes.

Giving up outside work for full-time homemaking is another way to shift gears. It also requires the same close study that other home work does.

Many of the issues that face women who bring outside work into their homes—the need for social contact, for order, for privacy, for structure—are issues for full-time homemakers as well.

Additionally, women who leave the labor force often experience a loss of external reinforcement about their value. Each of us needs to feel competent, and our culture doesn't reward the competencies we develop as full-time homemakers.

If we're going to make homemaking our career, we need an inner belief in its value and an ability to confirm and celebrate our competencies, even if nobody else does. Anyone who feels tempted to call herself "just a housewife" may not be a good candidate for this role as a full-time job.

The brilliance of Monday morning quarterbacks lies in their knowledge of how every play turned out. Life doesn't do us such favors.

Sometimes we can't know what is right for us without trying it. No matter how well we know our hearts, there is wisdom we acquire only *after* we act on our longings.

If working from home is a recurring heartsong, try it if you possibly can. Seek out ways to give home work a trial run without staking your welfare on it:

- *Ask if your employer will let you work from home one day a week.*
- *Cut back your hours and launch your new venture part-time.*

❦ Take a leave of absence and give it your all for three months.

When we drive through the mountains, we constantly shift upward and downward, seeking the right rpm for the grade that we're on. Life, too, is a series of grades, some steeper, some flatter. If we can shift gears as we travel over them, the trip will be smoother and safer.

> *We're told everybody gains when people work at home. . . . If all this is true, some of us must be doing it wrong.*

> JANET SIMONS AND WENDY UNDERHILL
> Contributors, *The Rocky Mountain News*

TANGLED
CONNECTIONS

Studies of women who work outside their homes reveal that many consider the relationships they form on the job to be the chief personal benefit of working.

For busy women, the workplace provides the most effortless opportunity to connect with other women. At work, we readily find the time and easy proximity that help casual relationships to grow deeper and richer.

Yet when women called my radio show with job-related dilemmas, the tangled connections they experienced at work were right at the top of their lists.

Gift-giving rituals that stretch patience and the pocketbook. Shifting dynamics when a promotion puts one friend over the other. The sheer energy that goes into maintaining friendship on the job. Abusive bosses. Toxic colleagues.

The time and proximity that are so helpful to nurture healthy connections at the same time leave us vulnerable to complicated or even destructive ones. When this occurs, the balance of social satisfaction tips, and a place we hoped would enrich our lives turns into one more bog that pulls us down.

It's tempting to underestimate the power of these complexities. After all, we say, this is just a job.

We need to be a little more compassionate with ourselves. The truth is, we do more than *work* with our work mates. We all but *live* with them several days a week.

In a real sense, our work mates form an intricate extended family system with the same potential for bringing us pleasure . . . or pain.

As we strive to simplify our work life and harmonize it with our personal life, it helps to remember that a boss is not just a boss. A coworker is not just a coworker. An employee is not just an employee. In the way we interact with them and the impact they have upon us, each is the equivalent of a parent, a sibling, an offspring.

The manner that we and they exercise authority and respond to it in birth families will color the way it is played out in our work families. The issues of competition and fairness that we wrestle with in sibling relationships will surface with our workplace peers.

Proximity makes it inevitable that we will feel the impact of the personal history and experience our coworkers bring to the job. If someone who reports to us grew up in a torrent of criticism, we may feel the impact of that upbringing when we supervise her. If our office mate is going through a family crisis, we may find our workload heavier because she is distracted.

Scenarios such as these are not *probabilities,* they are *realities,* and we have little or no ability to change them. If they are realities that feel like bonds, what we want is to manage the effect they have upon us.

One of the ways we can manage work mate connections is to beware of graduating them into friendships. A collegial relationship involves a well-defined, contained level of involvement; a friendship typically blurs those boundaries.

When boundaries fade, the interaction that once consisted of discussing work now inevitably expands to keeping up with personal issues. Simple actions, like walking out the door alone at lunchtime, can become problematic. Holidays arrive with another name on our gift lists.

Clear professional judgments can become clouded. What if our friend is cheating at her work or unloading it on us? What if only one of us gets promoted or comes under fire from a supervisor? It complicates our lives when these events take place beneath the overlay of friendship.

I have formed some of my closest friendships in the petri dish of work. Especially when we move to a new community, our workplace may be the most likely place to find new friends. If, however, we are already having trouble nourishing ourselves and outside friendships, adding new connections at work can become a burden.

As we consider the social possibilities of work, we need to ask ourselves . . .

> *Is there room in my personal life for another friend?*
>
> *Is there room in my workplace for more than the work at hand?*

If the answer to either of these is *No,* our task is to resist the temptation of promoting collegial relationships into something more by . . .

❦ KEEPING CONVERSATION OUT OF THE PERSONAL ARENA.

127
Sharing feelings and private experiences implies closeness. We set boundaries on work relationships when we take care about how far into the personal arena we venture.

When I arrive at the office after the weekend, I look forward to exchanging movie notes and dining adventures with anyone in my work family, but it is the unusual and rare colleague with whom I share more.

At the same time, I take care about how I handle my colleagues' excursions into the personal. When a work mate makes disclosures that imply a closeness I don't feel comfortable encouraging, I choose words that express empathy without inviting further discussion.

Gosh, that's unfortunate; I hope you can work it out, lets the speaker know *I heard you, and I understand.*

Gee, that's awful! What happened? opens the door to further disclosure and the claims that come with shared secrets.

❦ KEEPING ACTIVITIES IN THE PROFESSIONAL ARENA.

As soon as we invite (or accept an invitation) to lunch or to a drink after work or to a picnic on the weekend, we move our connection out of the workplace and onto our personal ground. Just like sharing feelings and personal experiences, this suggests a closer level of intimacy.

We can't control what other people want from their relationships with us. We *do* have control over how we respond to their overtures. I'm not suggesting that we never allow our workplace relationships to wander beyond the job, just that it is worthwhile to be aware of the complexities that emerge from our responses to "simple" invitations.

When we are the ones in the supervising position, maintaining personal distance becomes particularly problematic.

Being a boss is isolating for men and women alike because it means we have fewer peers on the job. When we are the only female at a supervisory level, the isolation tends to be magnified. The loneliness we feel may compound the standard temptation to befriend our work mates.

We need to realize at these moments that trying to be sister or mother to a flock of employees creates an illusion of connection but not necessarily the real thing. The undercurrent of unequal power is inescapable and makes an equal relationship difficult to achieve.

Indeed, all the nuances that characterize workplace relationships are amplified when they take place between an employee and her supervisor. The impact of these tangles is worth considering *before* forging ahead.

Sometimes we don't realize that a collegial relationship has moved to a more intimate level until after the evolution is complete. When this occurs and we feel that we've gotten ourselves into a relationship that is more than we can handle at work, we need to find words and actions that allow us to back away kindly.

We may need to take our work mate aside and say to her . . .

*I'm feeling spread a little thin right now. I'm
afraid I need to back off and get my work under
control.*

*This well feels especially dry right now. I wish I
could be of help to you, but I'm not in a place where
I have much to offer.*

*I've found that dwelling on the problems my
husband and I are having isn't helping me solve
them. It would be better for me if I let it rest for
a while.*

Workplace friendships, especially when they are young, are
planted in relatively shallow soil. When we back off, they often
dry up of their own accord.

Perhaps the most troublesome of workplace connections is the
toxic one—a boss or a coworker with problems so severe that
they poison the entire workplace. We don't have to be close to
these work mates to feel their effects; their very presence makes
work and life harder to handle.

I have found two approaches to the toxic work mate that
offer the most relief:

LIMIT CONTACT WITH THE PERSON.

We need to manage our exposure to poisonous coworkers by
setting and maintaining firm boundaries. If the toxic colleague is
a chronic complainer, for example, we can respond to her ap-
pearance in our work cubicle by saying, *"I only have five minutes*

to talk," and then ending the conversation when those five min-utes have elapsed.

❧ FIND A MODEL AND COPY HER OR HIM.

If we look around, it is possible we will find someone else in the workplace who appears to be working reasonably well with the toxic colleague. Search out that person, find out the secret to her or his success, and copy it. This tactic is especially useful when the toxic person is the boss, with whom it may be impractical to limit contact.

Workplaces set the stage for intimacy. When our spirits are starved for connection, it is natural to reach for the windfall of potential friends that comes our way in the normal course of daily activities.

Those workplace connections that feed our souls lighten the rest of the load we are carrying. They give us cause to rejoice. If we can remember that the best of these connections results when we choose with care and encourage with patience, then we may realize their full potential for making our work lives simpler.

> *Be courteous to all but intimate with few, and let those few be well tried before you give them your con-fidence. True friendship is a plant of slow growth and must undergo and withstand the shocks of ad-versity before it is entitled to the appellation.*

> ❧ GEORGE WASHINGTON

VI

SIMPLIFYING
OUR
FRIENDSHIP
LIFE

HOW OUR
GARDENS GROW

Of all that our hearts shelter, our friendships are among the most cherished.

Women find good friends to be one of life's essentials, a requirement so deep and so natural that we rarely question it. When our commitments and obligations overwhelm us, friends can buoy us and keep us afloat, even in the worst of times. That's why we feel so bereft when we have no time for our good friends, or find what time we have occupied by acquaintances we don't treasure. Without good friends, we feel unconnected.

Our longing for friends is a healthy hunger. It produces some of life's richest relationships. Yet to fully enjoy them, our challenge is finding a way to tend our friendship gardens with so many other things clamoring for our attention.

We are all born with the need for human connection, but from earliest childhood, each sex seeks to satisfy the need in unique ways.

A look at any elementary school yard finds the boys out on the playing field, noisily enjoying one another as they make rules for their heated competition and then parting company without regret when the game is over.

On their own playing field, the girls are also enjoying each other, but rule-making and competition tend to be subplots. The real agenda is making, nurturing, and keeping friends. It is the girls, not the boys, who worry about hurting the feelings of a competitor they defeat.

The rewards for success at making personal connections are great. We can all remember the relief and jubilation of being invited to a birthday party or the desolation of being left out. Having friends gives us a sense of enormous well-being, as if the world has scooped us into its cosmic embrace. We feel that we *belong*.

Unfortunately, this healthy need to connect and belong tends to become confused with the less useful belief that it is important to be liked by everyone. In our quest for approval, we operate on the principle that if some friends are good, lots are better, and we carry this playground wisdom into our friend-making for the rest of our lives.

In this way, our friendship gardens grow and fill, until nothing is really flourishing and new growth has no chance to take root. In our fear of friendlessness, we bring our fears to life by making our gardens so crowded there is no room for the new prize friendships that would bloom if only there were space.

We can't talk about simplifying our lives without looking at our friends.

We need intimate friends and casual friends, mates for our souls and buddies for the bench at our kids' swim meets. But we don't have a lot of time for people who take more out of our busy lives than they add.

Into what little free time we have, we must wedge whatever romance, leisure, and self-renewal we're going to know. Friendships take time and energy. Friends complicate our lives, and we have to be brave in weighing the cost of these complications.

We must look at the women we call friends and be honest with ourselves and with them about whether the moments we spend with them are enriching or impoverishing. In an unhurried life, a friendship garden that requires a lot of time just because it contains so many varieties doesn't pose much of a problem. But we're not living unhurried lives, and even one hour a month spent with someone whose company leaves us feeling annoyed or trapped or empty is one hour too many.

As young children, we all possess an uncanny and unnerving ability to assess the motives and sincerity of others. We may add friends pell-mell, but in our early years, we shed them with the same abandon.

What we need as adults is to reclaim those instincts and use them to evaluate our friendship gardens, weeding where we must. It is a daunting task because it asks us to face down some of our deepest fears.

It is by no means an impossible one.

> *Tell me what company thou keepest, and I'll tell thee what thou art.*

> MIGUEL DE CERVANTES
> *Don Quixote*

KEEPERS

I can remember being in graduate school and thinking how overwhelmed I was with work. Actually, I know now that I had a life of leisure compared to the years since. I know it was leisure because I had space for a number of interesting women in my life. More than that, I actually had time to spend with them.

On one particularly contemplative afternoon, I was thinking about a weekend dinner coming up and realized I was full of warm anticipation. I started musing about the varieties of women in my life and how each relationship had a life of its own. I found myself idly doodling, jotting down the qualities I liked about each woman.

I was taking advanced statistics at the time and charts seemed so orderly that I ended up making a chart. This was years ago, but I can still picture it perfectly.

I wrote lists of names in each of several columns, deferring classification until I discovered what the columns produced. When all the names were listed, I found they fell into five neat little categories:

1. Soul mates—friends who would be around forever

2. Friends who weren't close enough to fall under column 1 but with whom I strongly wished to stay in touch

3. Friends I knew only slightly but who exhibited potential for moving up to column 2 or 1

4. Friends with whom I spent lots of time but who I felt would eventually drift away

5. Friends whose place in my life had already begun to diminish

My serendipitous exercise turned out to be unexpectedly enlightening. The very moment I finished the chart, I knew whose presence in my life was elemental and whose presence was not.

When we go fishing, we throw back the fish that are small so they can grow to maturity. The rest we call the "keepers." Simplifying our friendships is not dissimilar. We free the friends who aren't right for us so they may move on to other, more appreciative connections, and we hold on to the ones that are just right.

My own road to a simpler friendship life began on that contemplative afternoon. I have never again made a chart like the one that emerged that day, but in other ways, I have continued to examine friendships in the hopes of finding the keepers among them.

A few years back, I was given a gift certificate for a wardrobe consultation. I was doing a lot of television appearances at the time, and one thing I knew about television was that I needed to look perfect. Now, I am not the perfect-looking type, so I was eager to have someone help me go through my closet and pitch the things that emphasized my imperfections.

I scheduled the consultation when my sister, Nancy, one of my soul mates, was to be in town, and I casually mentioned the project to Jan, a work mate with whom I had let the collegial boundaries blur.

Jan thought the project sounded intriguing and asked if she could come and watch.

I froze inside.

Watch? Watch me relive all the sizes I had occupied over the years? Watch me hold up those tired and boring clothes I couldn't part with? I simply couldn't imagine her witnessing such an event.

It was clear in that instant that Jan was a valued colleague but not a friend. The fact that, in the end, her attendance at my closet-cleaning didn't really bother me didn't change the recognition of her standing in my heart.

How we feel when we expose our insecurities to a friend helps us recognize the nature of that friendship. When we feel safe, it's a good sign.

If taking a risk with a friend doesn't reveal the truth about the friendship, the acid test is taking a trip with her. On the road, each and every annoying habit is exposed. Our ability to accept these habits—and have ours accepted—is a clue to the true depth of the relationship.

My friend Nora accepted the invitation of a soul mate to drive cross-country with the woman and her two young children, Greg and Natalie. For a year, the friends planned their adventure in elaborate and loving detail.

Finally, departure day dawned, and the travelers crawled into the minivan in high spirits. Within a few hours, however, total silence settled over the adults.

It had suddenly hit them both that there was no way they could spend twenty-two days locked in a car with a three-year-old and a six-year-old and feel the same about each other when the journey was over. They hadn't intended it, but they were giving their friendship the acid test.

Their relationship passed the test; a true friendship can usually recover from the trauma of negotiating a vacation together. But many friendships run aground at this or some other critical juncture, leaving us in the uneasy position of deciding what to do next.

Acknowledging that a friendship is limited or, worse, doomed, and acting on it, are two different matters.

The minute we consider backing away from a friendship, our playground fears and instincts are reactivated and compounded with the prospect of the unthinkable: telling another woman we cannot be her friend.

Yet acting on the recognition that a friendship is over is the essence of filling our lives with keepers, however sad it may be.

There are a number of approaches to this painful job. My close friend Dianne chose a stunningly direct one.

She had become acquainted with a woman named Brenda, and they were in contact regularly. Brenda wanted much more from their relationship than Dianne had the time or interest to offer. One winter afternoon, Dianne was feeling queasy about Brenda's eager invitations to spend time together. At last, she acknowledged her own lack of interest in the relationship and decided to act on it.

"You know, when I look at our friendship, I am aware it isn't satisfying to me," she told Brenda. "I know we talk about getting together more, but when I look at where I decide to spend my time, I realize our time together is less and less a priority for me. I think there is a message here. You deserve a friend who has the same level of interest."

Brenda was disappointed but also a little relieved. In fact, she had seen the signs of Dianne's flagging interest but had chosen to ignore them.

As hard as candor sounds—and is—it may be the kindest way to handle such friends. If we have any respect for these women at all, it is more generous to admit our lack of commitment than to subject them to a campaign of slights until they discover our disinterest themselves.

Realistically, this level of candor may be initially unattainable. In our efforts to avoid conflict and hurt feelings, we may find ourselves falling back on passive techniques—unreturned notes and telephone calls, even a change of schedule that reduces our contact with the person.

These strategies may distance us from the friend, but they do so at a cost. Being honest is harder at the front end, but it allows us to walk away cleanly. Avoidance looks easier, but it leaves a trail of misunderstanding and ill will that muddies our sense of accomplishment.

If total candor is too daunting, there are other honest ways to retreat from a friendship.

✦ TAKE SOME TIME OFF.

Tell your friend—or friends—that you need to step back and evaluate how you're spending your time. Then back away and take a look at what you see. As with many other facets of our lives, sometimes we need distance to gain perspective. Whether we feel loss or relief once we step back, we have discovered something about that friendship.

✦ ACT ON YOUR DISCOVERY.

If you find that you feel more relief than loss as a result of your time off, you need to act on that discovery or the friendship will continue to be a claim upon your limited time. Explain that you've thought things over and need to make some changes in the way you pass your time, perhaps to spend more with family or pursuing hobbies.

✦ HONOR YOUR COMMITMENT.

Friends have a way of easing back into our lives despite our best efforts to reduce our contact with them. Be ready to field telephone calls that test your boundaries. Sometimes, it is helpful to even rehearse what we will say:

> *Thanks for your call. This is a hard time for me,*
> *but I feel I have to honor my commitment to my*
> *other projects.*

✦ BE PREPARED FOR THE PAIN OF LETTING GO.

When the desire to let go or scale down a friendship is not reciprocal, you may hurt your friend's feelings, a repercussion that will probably feel unpleasant. Even if the parting is without that pain, you may feel a loss. At these times, it will help to remind yourself how awful it felt to be spread too thin and how good it feels to have time for the people you cherish.

As wise as it is to contain our friendship gardens, it is advisable to take time about doing it.

We need to remember it is not always spring. There are times in our lives when we cannot be available to our friends, or when they are not available to us. It is important to distinguish when a lull in a friendship is simply a season that will pass.

We need to acknowledge that there are conflicts between friends—betrayal, dishonesty, unkind or thoughtless remarks in a time of need—and differentiate the momentary lapses from the fundamental flaws. I have seen more women in therapy who wished they had repaired friendships than women who wished they had been more final. It may be wiser to err on the side of acceptance than to lose a fine friend as a result of impatience or intolerance.

We need to be patient. Think of the bulbs and seeds we plant in our gardens. It takes time for them to germinate and reach full growth. Friendships are no different. Give them the time they need to become what they can.

One of the discouraging possibilities we may make when we weed our friendship gardens is that we don't really have many people in our lives that we consider to be keepers. In our rare, spare moments, it is worthwhile to figure out what types of friends we would like to have. As new people enter our lives, we can use that information to help us spot the potential keepers among them.

We all need a soul mate or two, but there are many kinds of

keepers—friends with whom we share our history, friends who make us laugh. One friend may just make us feel great about ourselves. Who couldn't use a cheerleader now and again? Another may help us remember what matters.

We need them all, but we may have them only if we have cleared a space for them in the garden.

> *The loneliest woman in the world is a woman without a close woman friend.*

TONI MORRISON
American writer

CELEBRATION

The enormous effort of weeding our friendship gardens is not fully rewarded unless we make time to savor the results.

Try to spend at least a few minutes of every week with one of the keepers in your life. It doesn't matter whether you connect by telephone or over a glass of wine or simply exchange a brief, loving note. In connecting, you celebrate your friendship and nourish its strength.

QUARTETS
VERSUS
DUETS

Individual friends, as delightful as they are, do not complete our friendship gardens. Our lives most likely will also include couples and, especially if we have children, possibly whole families as well.

Couple friendships are innately different from individual friendships. It is harder to form four-way bonds of equal strength, so these friendships rarely seem as passionate as our one-on-one relationships. And because couple connections often grow from circumstances that can change—where we work, where we live, whom our children play with—they often have a more obvious seasonal quality.

Maybe as a result, we tend to be more casual about couple friendships. If individual friendships are the seeds we plant with hope and lovingly nurture to maturity, couple friendships are the potted plants we pick up in the grocery store because they catch our eye and we figure they can be added to the scenery without a great deal of effort.

We're so casual about couple friendships that we find more than one way to run amok: We may have so many that they become just another source of stress, or we may skip them altogether, reluctant to add one more feature to an already crowded landscape.

As we strive for more balanced lives, I believe there is a special place for other couples. I have seen their value to couples in therapy, and I have enjoyed it in my own life.

Couple relationships offer friendship dividends that are unique. They give us membership in a *community* of affection and a frame of reference for assessing our own partnerships. If we are single, they can function as a sort of surrogate family, giving us not only sisters but brothers, too, and a place to "audition" our own prospective partners before a caring audience whose vision isn't hormone-blurred.

Being with couples can take some of the pressure off our own partnerships—a big plus, since no spouse can meet all needs. And if the pair is happily joined, it can show us how the dicey business of life partnership is done.

Perhaps best of all, other couples become part of the fabric of our own families. At both the celebrations and the lamentations of life, at the births and the deaths and all the markers in between, they become woven into our own histories, a large and reassuring circle of arms around us.

Yet for all their satisfactions, successful quartets are difficult to form and maintain. What we need are strategies for minimizing the difficulties so we can maximize the rewards.

The logistics of foursomes can be mind-boggling. Line up the work schedules, travel plans, and social obligations of four individuals—much less six or eight—and what we're likely to find is a calendar without a single open date for months running.

One strategy is marking out time for couple dates on the calendar *first* and then planning around them.

Another winning strategy when both couples have children is including the whole family, which provides couple time without taking us away from the kids.

I think my friend DeAnne has the most practical strategy of all. Instead of planning couple dates with their favorite couple friends, she and her husband, John, make them spontaneously on short notice.

"We do have some couple friends that we schedule way in advance, but we don't see them as often because it's easier to be spontaneous," says DeAnne.

"We work hard all week, and I want a weekend that is easy. If I book too far in advance, then I feel pressured when our date finally rolls around—like I had plenty of time to plan something wonderful."

Of course, spontaneity only works when we're available to be spontaneous. Taking a big black marker and crossing out several days a week or a month to see what unfolds does wonders for serendipity.

As formidable as they are, logistics are not the biggest obstacle to couple friendships. The personal dynamics are even more likely to bog us down.

One of the complaints I hear from women who want couples in their lives is that their husbands aren't nearly as interested in couple friendships as they are. (Not surprisingly, I don't hear men complain that their wives aren't interested.) Since doubles can't be played with three people, this situation may require some negotiating.

Couples in this bind can benefit from looking at what each of them is already asking of each other.

Perhaps the husband is in a job that requires the wife to attend social functions she doesn't relish. Or he's a sports nut and she's not, but he wants her to come with him to the games.

I suggest cutting a deal:

> *I'll be cheerful about the hockey matches if you'll be*
> *cheerful about spending some time each month*
> *going out with friends.*

Perhaps the husband is already spending time for the wife's sake in an obligatory activity that she would be willing to swap for some couple time:

> *Okay, I'll go alone, or with a friend, or skip my*
> *subtitled foreign films altogether if you'll agree to a*
> *date with friends instead.*

It's usually easier to give up something if we're getting something we want in exchange.

Then there are the problems of matching interests, values, and lifestyle and avoiding competitiveness and jealousy.

In a one-on-one friendship, all we need is one other person with whom we feel a connection. In foursomes, each individual needs to be able to connect at a satisfactory level with two other people in addition to his or her own partner. This is an area where, if we value couples in our lives, we may have to make some concessions to reality.

Over the years, my husband, Pat, and I have had a number of couple friendships we maintained even though we weren't equally excited about the couple. We maintained them because we want the benefits of having couples in our lives and because we have agreed to try to honor those relationships that are most important to each other. At the same time, we each reserve the right to cry "uncle" if the relationship simply becomes intolerable.

We have agreed that we don't have to *love* all the members of our quartets; we just have to *like* each other well enough to enjoy the time we spend together.

Just as significant to our couple friendships are the sea changes that come upon us, altering our lives in such fundamental ways that our connections are weakened, sometimes beyond repair. We have all probably suffered through the effects of a separation or divorce on a foursome, but other life changes also can affect couple connections.

I remember taking a difficult radio call several years ago from a woman whose husband's job had been a victim of Denver's then sinking economy. Suddenly, they no longer could afford the dinners and theater outings they had once shared with their couple friends. Beyond that, being with other men who were still working depressed the husband further about his own situation.

Their friends, not wanting to lose the couple, offered to treat the couple on their joint outings, but that did not solve the problem. Their shared circumstances had altered, and the friendships could not survive the new environment.

Another couple comes to mind who thoroughly enjoyed a neighbor couple until the pair moved across town. Driving a half-hour for a get-together was so much more complicated than shouting a dinner invitation over the fence that the families, once so close, drifted apart.

At times like these, it is helpful to remember that just as we have a need for all sorts of individual friends, we have a need for different kinds of couple friends. A few are the equivalent of soul mates, couples with whom the four-way bonds are so strong that they overcome crisis, distance, and major life changes. Far more are friendships that meet a need or serve a purpose for a season.

It is important to recognize when the season is over, when changing circumstances make the obstacles to the relationship too high to surmount. Thankfully, this is often much easier than in our individual relationships. As meaningful as they are, our complex couple friendships are so fragile that the ties loosen more readily than not.

Whatever the obstacles, we know that couples are important to us when we experience dismay over the departure of one we found rewarding. I remember the day the FOR SALE sign went up at the house of cherished neighbor friends. I was heartbroken, as if a hole had been torn in the fabric of my own life.

When we find ourselves longing for the satisfactions we found in the company of couple friends and nowhere else, it is a signal. We need to find a way to bring couples into our lives or to raise our investment in the ones who are already among us.

When we are thinking about the things we're thankful for and grateful for, there's hardly anything greater than good friends and long-time relationships who make it possible to be gathered at a time like this and share our happiness.

WEDDING TOAST TO THE MARRIAGE OF AMY HOCART AND WILLIAM GOLDY JR.

ROOM
AT
THE INN?

Whenever I read 19th-century novels, I am awed by the picture of hospitality they paint. Because transportation made travel such an ordeal, guests who went to the trouble of visiting could be expected to stick around for weeks—even months.

If we have moved from our roots or been left behind by loved ones who have, we can expect that our friends, too, eventually will materialize as houseguests, although more likely for a few days than for weeks or months.

When we have time and space for them, these visits can be renewing beyond compare. Sharing meals, outings, and late-night chats gives a dimension to friendship and a break from the daily grind that a mere lunch date can't offer.

But when we are already running as fast as we can and are

still falling behind, the elated announcement from friends that they are coming to stay can also produce a monumental case of ambivalence.

Once we know how much friends matter to us and have found the keepers among individuals and couples alike, we still have to decide how much access to ourselves we can wisely grant within the limits of our time and energy.

And if we decide to limit the access, we must learn how to do it gently to preserve our connections through the fences we feel compelled to build.

My boss stopped by my house shortly after my youngest son was born, and I'm relieved I wasn't there.

His gesture was kind, but I would have been mortified to find him on my doorstep, even if I hadn't been running around in sweats with a protective diaper thrown over my shoulder. He just didn't belong in my home.

On the other hand, there was an engineer at the radio station who showed up with a piece of wedding cake because he knew it was a special weakness of mine. I was thrilled. Although we had never socialized outside of work, he belonged there.

When our homes are our sanctuaries, it behooves us to take care whom we allow in, especially when the visitor arrives with suitcase in hand.

My mother-in-law, Peg, could arrive at any hour of any day and be welcome for as long as we could entice her to stay because a wake of peace follows wherever she goes.

On the other hand, I have cherished friends whose arrival fills me with apprehension because they need or expect more than I can provide.

Friends or family members who move into our physical

space can be a bit like Alice after she ate the cake that turned her into a giant: They suddenly fill up every inch.

When friends who may come to stay are a feature in our lives, we need to ask ourselves . . .

Am I up for this?

Some people don't ever want people in their homes; others want to be the nation's innkeeper.

For most of us, the ability and willingness to have house-guests comes and goes with the times of life. It's easier when we're young and unencumbered and harder when we're up at night with babies. Specific circumstances, like beginning a new job or relocating or another important life event, may affect our ability to enjoy the presence of extras in our home.

With so much clamoring for our attention, we need to be honest with ourselves about whether we are in a season where visitors are truly welcome.

My friend Lynn found this out the hard way when she hosted a houseguest for three weeks during a particularly busy period of her life. As she departed, the guest announced that she had never realized how selfish Lynn was.

I know Lynn well enough to know she is not selfish. She was just in a season when her house had spare room but her life didn't.

Even when we have room in our lives to share our homes, we need to go on to ask . . .

Is this a friend I can enjoy as an overnight guest?

I think we all have friends we adore but couldn't stand living with, even for a weekend. I have a dear friend with whom I have taken a weekend trip every summer since our children were born. We travel together exceptionally well except on one count: It takes me twenty minutes to get ready for the world, but it takes her two hours. This is fine for our lazy weekend getaways, but I don't think it would wear well if she were my houseguest.

Personal space is also an issue. Some of us need more of it than others. When guests don't understand where our internal boundaries are set, it gives us the same uneasy sensation we get from people who insist on standing just a few inches too close when they speak with us. It feels uncomfortable.

We may not know our friends aren't compatible guests the first time they come to stay, but we have no excuse the next time they call.

When we look forward to a friend's visit with pleasure rather than dread, we can take that as an encouraging sign. Yet unless we're living a life of leisure, we probably need to find ways to simplify the hostess role. We need to ask . . .

How can I make this easier?

To answer this question, we have to start with an admission about what makes having guests a bit of a trial for us. Is it that they upset our routines or that we can't face taking the cog railway to the top of Pike's Peak one more time? Is it the cooking or the changing of all the beds after they leave that does us in?

If we know what makes hosting difficult, we know where to start simplifying. Then we need to be straightforward:

> *I would love to see you and the kids, but getting dinner on the table just about does me in. How about if I spring for take-out two nights and you cook the other two?*

When the idea of asking more of our guests or offering less is un-appealing, we may want to explore whose expectations are the problem. Is it the guest's expectations that are unrealistic or our own? Sometimes we do what we think people want when they don't really want it.

There is one friend I love but never visit without a sense of ambivalence because of the extremes to which she takes her hospitality. Instead of being able to relax and enjoy her, I feel like a burden, and that makes me feel guilty. Sometimes I just prefer to stay in a hotel.

If we can ferret out our own driving expectations, we often do ourselves *and* our guests a favor.

On the other hand, if the guest's expectations are the problem, we need to attack them head-on.

I have a woman friend who occasionally calls to say she's coming to town. What she doesn't say—but what I know—is that she also wants my undivided attention when she arrives.

To avoid tensions when she gets here, I now send her a copy of my schedule for the days she plans to visit. *This is what's already on my schedule and can't be changed,* I tell her. *I would love for you to come knowing the time that I have available.*

When we tell guests the truth about our availability, some will accept it and others will protest.

When they object, we have to ask ourselves, *Who's problem is this anyway?* If the friend can't roll with our tide, maybe something essential is missing in the friendship, or maybe the friend just isn't the guest for us.

And for that special category of guests, the ones who buy the tickets and *then* call to say they're on the way, I recommend a list of hotel phone numbers close at hand. Yes, it may be impossible to dispense it without a twinge of guilt, but I figure that helping them out with reservations is a great deal more thoughtful than booking a flight and expecting that my door will be open.

Setting limits on our houseguests sets off so many barking dogs that many of us are tempted to solve the issue by just skipping them altogether.

I counsel caution on this count unless you happen to be someone who really never enjoys having guests around.

As disruptive as they may be, houseguests can actually normalize life. If they belong to that special category of *ideal* guest, they even make things *better*.

I once had a houseful of friends from Germany at a time when my career had taken a lurch on the roller-coaster. They were the best possible thing that could have happened. They gave me something much more pleasurable to think about than my crisis, and they gave of themselves in a way that nourished me at a time of genuine need.

Many houseguests are a bonus to have around. My friend Lynn's next long-term houseguest couldn't wait to sit down and help the kids with their homework every night. Lynn prayed she would never leave, and the guest loved her stay.

When distance has intervened in a friendship, playing the hostess may be essential to keeping the relationship alive over the miles. As long as we keep an eye on the edges of the stage, we may well find the role to be one of our most gratifying.

> *Do not neglect to show hospitality to strangers, for by*
> *this some have entertained angels without knowing it.*

HEBREWS 13:2

VII

SIMPLIFYING
OUR FAMILY
LIFE

HUSBANDS
NEED
NOT APPLY

A few years ago, Rupert Holmes had a hit song about a man and woman who, bored with their "old dull routine," set off secretly in search of someone new through the personal ads. Each wrote of longing to share piña coladas, get caught in the rain, and make love at midnight.

When they reached the rendezvous negotiated through the newspaper, the man and woman, of course, found each other. It turned out they already had the right mates; they had just allowed themselves to forget all the delight they had once taken from one another.

The quality of our intimate lives is one of the major casualties of our over-full days.

As demands on us increase, and we search for the time and

energy to meet them, most of us end up stealing it from our intimate lives. We fool ourselves into thinking we can do without the leisurely sharing that fosters closeness, and that just living under the same roof and grabbing an occasional private moment will be enough.

It is not.

If we choose to marry, we are acknowledging that sharing life with a partner matters to us, that we want to participate in life's joys and disappointments with a primary loved one at our side. When things don't work out that way, we feel a loss at our very core.

Few of our marriages are candidates for simplification. Chances are, in our efforts to meet our many competing obligations, we have already *oversimplified* them, stripping them down to the barest of essentials. We may have grown so distant that we feel more like roommates than life partners.

On the road to simpler yet fuller lives, our husbands are what the English call a "roundabout," a place where we may circle around and head back in the direction from which we came. We need to make *more* of our marriages, not less of them, despite all the other demands upon us, even if the effort seems at first just another complication.

I once attended a conference where one of the speakers asked the audience, "Have you ever played boat?"

"Boat," he went on to explain, is a game for couples having difficulty finding time for their partnership.

It begins by raiding the refrigerator, gathering some delectables (romantic varieties preferred), perhaps picking up a couple of unread magazines, and retreating to the bed.

Which becomes the boat.

"The idea," he explained, "is that the two of you are on a boat surrounded by water and for whatever time period you've set aside, you cannot get off the boat."

What happens in the boat is entirely up to the players, but however the time is spent, it will assuredly be more delicious than paying the bills or cleaning the bathrooms.

The boat game is only one of a thousand techniques for renewing an intimate connection, but I like it more than many of the alternatives because it is *playful.*

Fifteen hours into a typical day, what woman—or man, for that matter—wants to sit down and *work* on her marriage?

What we need as we try to recapture lost closeness is to learn from our kids, who are always finding ways to turn chores into games. Renewing our marriages when we feel perpetually wilted can seem like one more job. I suspect we would have more enthusiasm for the effort if we could find ways to make it feel more like play.

Fellow psychologists Wyndol Furman, Howard Markman, and I once conducted a survey on marital happiness in association with a Denver newspaper and KCNC, a local television station. The results offered a surprising revelation about the power of play.

Nearly 3,000 respondents returned the 138-question form that ran in the *Rocky Mountain News*'s Sunday magazine. When all the data were collected and analyzed, the three of us were astonished to find that one of the best predictors of marital happiness was the amount of *fun* a couple shared. Almost without exception, the happiest couples were the ones who reserved a significant place for play in their relationships with one another.

Nolan is one of our favorite houseguests because he has a

knack for turning up the level of fun in our lives. He once materialized in the kitchen to chop onions wearing a ski mask. If we seek out the simple ways to restore play to our marriages, we may well find ourselves enjoying them more.

When we start looking for places where a couple can share pleasure, the bedroom is an obvious one to consider. Unfortunately, with so many other things going on, many women and men alike have come to view sex as one more chore.

As a therapist, I used to hear from patients about impotence and problems achieving orgasm. Today, the chief complaint is about a fatigue so pervasive that it even has a name: inhibited sexual desire. It is widely regarded as the most common sexual dysfunction of our decade.

Our sexual connections with our mates are undeniably and hugely important, but with all the pressures we face daily, they require care in our reading of them.

Sex is sometimes seen as a barometer for the general health of our marriages, but it is helpful to remember that a barometer gives us more information than barometric pressure. It is true that emotional distance in our relationships can get reported in our sex lives, but the same may be said for chaos, fatigue, and a lot of other less ominous developments in our lives.

We need to be realistic about our sexual appetites and responses and careful about the meaning we take from our sexual lives. Especially in a household with children, where sex is the last item on the day's agenda, unbridled passion may not often be in the cards, if ever.

When this is troubling to us, we can benefit from looking at sex much as we have looked at so many other things, examining its place in our lives as partners.

✿ Does sex matter to us?

✿ How much does it matter?

✿ If it matters more to one of us that the other, how can we negotiate a compromise that meets both of our needs?

✿ What would it take for this to work?

If we say that sex matters and then don't find time for it, perhaps it doesn't matter as much as we thought, or maybe we have too many priorities and we need to move some of the others down the line.

Whatever its priority and our approach, sex benefits from a spirit of play. If we could anticipate having fun when we turn out the lights, we might not be so eager to go to sleep.

Like so much in life, marriage has its seasons. Times of incredible closeness and richness are interspersed with periods of distance and loneliness.

What we must do, if our marriages are important to us, is find ways to sustain the closeness even when circumstances temporarily reshuffle our priorities.

Some techniques have been tried enough that therapists and happily paired couples know them to be true. What follows here is by no means an exhaustive list, but it includes my personal favorites.

✿ GIVE REGULAR AIRTIME TO FEELINGS.

Nothing feels better or promotes closeness faster than being heard and feeling understood.

One highly effective technique for promoting closeness is called "active listening." Start by setting aside thirty inviolate minutes for sharing emotions. Let's assume you go first. Spend fifteen minutes talking about what feels important to you at the moment. Your partner's job is to *actively* listen and to demonstrate that he has heard by putting your feelings into his own words, without editorial comment, until you are satisfied that he has understood. Then it's his turn: He talks, and you reflect his feelings back to him. Most good couples manuals contain detailed discussions of this valuable technique.

❧ DATE YOUR HUSBAND.

Make a standing date for time to be alone and make sure that nothing preempts it. The date doesn't have to be for dinner and dancing; a long walk will do. The key is spending pleasurable time alone, focused on each other, with the emphasis on *pleasurable* and *alone*.

❧ SEEK CONVERSATIONAL TOPICS THAT LIFT YOU UP.

Instead of spending dinner talking over the office wars, talk about something you're looking forward to—the weekend, summer vacation, the holidays—or about a pleasurable memory from your shared past. Reframe the unmet desires you may be experiencing as dreams you want to share with him rather than as disappointments.

❧ PLAY "YOU BE ME AND I'LL BE YOU."

Trading places is one of the most powerful ways to break out of the rut of conflict reruns. Let's say you have stumbled over a perennial source of contention. Instead of having the usual dispute, each of you takes the other person's position (which, of course, you know by heart because you've heard it so many times). With all the flair and dramatics you can muster, do your mate's shtick. Then he gets to do yours.

Despite your best efforts to hold your position, it's almost impossible not to feel what the other person feels after dramatizing his position. And because this exercise produces caricatures of one another, it displaces some of the tension of the situation with humor.

✿ SPEND TIME WITH COUPLES WHO ARE WELL MARRIED.

Couples who have already passed the spots where you are struggling, who like one another or who bring fun into your life, help to restore perspective to and refresh married life. Seek them out and treasure your time with them.

And, by all means, find ways to play with your partner, whether it be "boat" or sharing piña coladas and getting caught in the rain.

> *Chains do not hold a marriage together. It is threads, hundreds of tiny threads which sew people together through the years. This is what makes a marriage last—more than passion or even sex!*
>
> ∽ SIMONE SIGNORET
> French actress

NOURISHING
THE
SEEDLINGS

I recently found myself negotiating with my youngest son, Michael, about his summer vacation.

Did he want to attend art camp or sports camp or Cabin Camp, a perennial favorite in the foothills of the Rockies?

Finally, he said, "You know, Mom, I don't want to do any camps. Last summer went so fast. I think it's because I did too much."

Bull's eye.

Children's requirements are really pretty simple.

Kids for the most part want and need our warmth and consistency and love. They want us to be near them and *with* them—not merely in the same room while on the telephone talking to somebody else. If they're still fairly young, they want us to play with them.

And what are we giving them?

Love, yes, but that's just the beginning.

We are so anxious to make sure they get "enough" or "the best" that we turn them into another "job," overloading their young lives just as surely as we overload our own.

We don't put much stock in our own maternal "instincts," whatever those are. Instead, we feel dogged by a lack of self-confidence. Living in an information-driven society, we turn to books and experts and classes for guidance and forget to consult with our hearts and the spirits of our own children.

Our motives are worthy: We want to raise happy, productive children. And some of our choices are driven by necessity. If we have to work, for example, that limits our options in countless ways.

But what we've missed in the process is what's conveyed in the old truism *You can't get there from here.* The more we're working and scheduling and running around, the less the kids are getting of what *they* really want and need.

We could all make raising children a great deal more simple if we would discover and honor what our children need by stopping the music long enough to ask . . .

> *Who is this child?*
> *What are her or his needs?*

Let's consider what we do for our children in light of what *they* need rather than basing it upon what we've been told they need, or what we need from them. I suspect we might learn that our kids don't want all the things that are absorbing so much of our time and energy.

There is so much that *has* to be done to raise children well—loving, instructing, feeding, clothing, nurturing, nursing. These are not negotiable. Music lessons, sports programs, enrichment classes, summer camp, play dates, sleep-overs, and a thousand other possibilities exist to keep us on the run, and they *are* negotiable. Children will reach adulthood without them, even productive adulthood.

When negotiable opportunities suit our children and when we can provide them without cheating on the nonnegotiable ones, they are worth pursuing. If the opportunities are inventions that don't match our children's natures and make our own days more hectic, we need to question why we're still doing them.

One of the most powerful ways we can simplify our lives as mothers is to step up the pace with which we're letting our children go.

By letting go, I don't mean abandoning limits. Our children need us to set limits, just as certainly as the most aggressive boxer in the ring needs the ropes that hold him in. It doesn't mean exposing them to danger. My kids don't have a choice about wearing bicycle helmets or seat belts. If they don't make the right choice, those are two choices I feel perfectly okay making for them.

It *does* mean being more selective about the limits *we* set, allowing *them* to make ever more choices and then to experience the consequences of those decisions.

For most mothers, "letting go" feels vague and even scary until we break it into its parts and examine each in turn.

Almost from their birth and virtually every day until they leave home, there are moments when we can hold on to our children or let them go. Whether they're six months or sixteen years, we can fret over what and how much they eat, when and where they go to bed, and endless other activities—or we can turn these choices over to our children.

Personally, I wrestle with the absence of vegetables in our home. Corn and mashed potatoes are the only vegetables my kids eat. Now, I can try to control this (*No vegetables, no dessert* and similar strategies are probably as old as vegetables themselves), or I can let go.

I've chosen to let go because I can do so without endangering my children and because I know that eventually they will eat foods that happen to be green.

Here is just a short list of other potential battlegrounds where we can manage our children or let them learn to manage themselves within the safety of our love:

BEDTIME (WEEKDAY, WEEKEND, HOLIDAY, SUMMER)

CLOTHES (STYLE, SIZE, COLOR, MESSAGE)

ETIQUETTE (TABLE, TELEPHONE, SOCIAL)

FOOD (HOW MUCH, WHAT KIND, WHEN, WHERE)

HAIR (LENGTH, COLOR, STYLE)

HOMEWORK (ENDLESS POSSIBILITIES)

MUSIC (TYPE, CONTENT, VOLUME, TIMING)

PERSONAL HABITS (EMISSIONS, EXPLOSIONS)

SHOWERING (HOW OFTEN, WHAT TIME, HOW LONG)

TELEPHONE (DITTO)

Our ability to turn over issues like these depends to some extent on our tolerance for the choices they make. It's not necessary to turn over everything, but we simplify parenthood when we begin to identify at least the battles we are doomed to lose or that aren't as important as others. The first time my son John drove the family car down the driveway and into the street alone, the issue of whether he brought in the trash cans felt a lot less important to me.

As we make these adjustments, our children begin to develop a sense of competence and self-confidence. At the same time, we reduce conflict and conserve our energy for more critical issues.

I remember as a new mother telling an experienced one, "I'm looking forward to when I can stop worrying about the baby choking to death on something he eats."

She laughed and shook her head. "It's not that easy," she said. "After that, there are sockets to worry about, and then tricycles and germs at preschool. You think you'll be relieved to stop worrying about him riding his bike in the street, but then he'll be in a car. It never ends."

When our children are born, they need our protection from just about everything, whether it's the over-friendly family dog or a chunk of finger food too large for their infant throats. As they grow, we continue to protect them, but our role as protector is under constant revision.

The hardest choices for us to leave to our children are the ones we know may result in pain or failure or even injury. I remember when John decided he wanted to play football. A knot formed in my stomach that didn't go away until the season ended with him still intact.

These are the lettings-go that most daunt us.

When we are tempted to make choices in order to spare our children the consequences of their own, we need to remind ourselves that we do them no great favors by running interference between them and life.

Adversity, as awful as it feels when we're experiencing it, is generally what gives us substance. When we find it hard to turn a choice over to our children because we remember the pain that a poor one caused us, perhaps we need to look further, at what we learned and how we grew. The strength those lessons taught us may give us courage to allow our children to gain their own.

It is the life work of children to emancipate themselves from their parents. Every single day, they are busy learning to take charge of their own lives. The more room we give them to do that, the more likely they are to grow up as the healthy, whole, productive adults we were all hoping for in the first place.

When we seek out the places where we can simply get out of the way, our youngsters find their work simplified.

So do we.

As a Denver Seminary student, Deb roomed for a semester with a family where the mother wrestled daily with the needs and demands of two supercharged kids.

One day, Deb turned to the mother and said, "By the way, I don't know whether you hear this often, but you are a very good mother."

The woman burst into tears. Deb's simple and kind words, rarely heard by this mother or by most mothers, were so unexpected and welcome that she was overcome.

We work hard to raise our children and care deeply about the results. Yet we feel so uncertain about our abilities and so unsure of the outcomes, we hear so little praise and so much criticism, that no matter what we do, we are haunted by self-doubt.

As mothers, we need to applaud ourselves and seek out the applause of others. We should savor every tribute because we deserve them, and we need all we can get.

I know a mother who closes her daughter's bedtime ritual every night by saying, *You're the best little girl in the whole world,* to which the daughter replies, *You're the best mommy in the whole world.* Even though the girl is not so little any more, both of them hug the words to their hearts, and the daughter's praise helps sustain the mother through other, more rugged hours.

Sadly, there are more people who are eager to let us know what we're doing wrong than what we're doing well. Even when they are silent, we seem to have an uncanny knack for *imagining* they are measuring us and then concluding we have come up short.

A mother I know is dedicated to finding every conceivable enrichment program for her son and making sure he doesn't miss out on a single one. She reports on her research in a way that leaves other mothers wondering if they have deprived their children of some incredible experience because they failed to *know* enough.

We are all prone to unproductive exercises such as this. With so much information available about the possibilities, we feel duty bound to duplicate everything that appears even marginally beneficial.

Just as we need to seek out applause, we do well to avoid subjecting ourselves to people or situations that exaggerate our self-doubts. Guilt is a sure detour off the road to a simpler life.

I once heard a speaker reminisce about her experience as a mother. She remembered gazing at her sleeping two-year-old and wondering how in the world she could ever face his growing up and leaving home.

That memory returned to her years later, at a particularly difficult time when her son was sixteen. Noting how her own attitude toward letting go had changed with her son, she concluded about motherhood, "God works in wondrous ways."

Our children are supposed to grow up and leave us. Those who don't end up as incomplete, unfulfilled adults. The more we allow their spirits to unfold within the safety of our love, the closer we come to the heart of motherhood.

> *At every step, the child should be allowed to meet the real experiences of life; the thorns should never be plucked from his roses.*

> ELLEN KEY
> Swedish writer

 RITUAL

Children and parents once assumed the kids would help out in the home. This is no longer true. In fact, household chores are a major battlefield in many families.

Yet children benefit from household responsibilities, and every woman could use an extra set of hands around the house. I suggest two strategies to mothers who are overworked and would like to stop being underwhelmed with the assistance they are getting from their children. (This also works with husbands, by the way.)

1. WHEN CHILDREN ARE QUITE YOUNG (SIX AND UNDER), THEY OFTEN LOVE TO HELP. IT'S NEVER TOO EARLY TO ENCOURAGE THIS HABIT. YOUNG CHILDREN THIS AGE CAN DUST, SORT CLEAN LAUNDRY, PICK UP TOYS.

2. OLDER CHILDREN WHO HAVE NEVER HELPED OFTEN RESIST WHEN THEY ARE FINALLY ASKED. IN THESE SITUATIONS, I RECOMMEND THAT EVERY MEMBER IN THE FAMILY KEEP A LIST OF THE CHORES SHE OR HE PERFORMS FOR THE HOUSEHOLD DURING THE COURSE OF A WEEK. AT A FAMILY MEETING WHEN THE WEEK HAS ENDED, EVERYONE COMPARES LISTS. IN MOST HOMES, MOM'S LIST IS HANDS-DOWN THE LONGEST. IN SOME FAMILIES, HERS IS THE ONLY LIST.

So it's time to divvy chores. This activity resembles choosing players for a school yard sports team. Each family member in turn selects one chore she or he is willing to do until Mom's list is reduced to her satisfaction.

If nobody volunteers for a specific chore, Mom declares that this job just won't be done. At first, nobody is alarmed with the idea that the dishes won't be washed. This tends to change when every dish in the house is sitting in the sink, dirty.

When jobs don't get done by their respective volunteers, I suggest saying, *I'll do my job as soon as you do yours.* So if the dog hasn't been fed, you say, *I'll get your dinner as soon as the dog gets hers.* Or if the dishwasher is still full of clean dishes, *I'll start dinner as soon as the dishwasher is empty.*

These tactics take some fortitude and perhaps a set of earplugs at first to weather the complaints, but they deliver a big payoff: With consistency, they do indeed work.

TENDING THE
OLD
GROWTH

Those among us whose parents let go judiciously while we were still under their watchful eye reap a bonus in adulthood: Already largely emancipated, we leave the family home relatively free of conflict and misgivings.

If not, this unfinished business awaits us.

Little on the road to a simpler life is more difficult to consider than our parents.

In them is embodied everything we ever were, are, or hoped to be. I cannot even watch my parents walk down a street and observe their gait and the way they move their arms without seeking myself and my siblings. Parents are mirrors in which we see our own reflections *everywhere*.

Yet there comes a time in each life for moving away from our parents and meeting them in a new place where we are all individuals rather than extensions of one another.

Some of us reach this place by the time we leave home. More of us work on it throughout adulthood. Sometimes, the process continues beyond our parents' deaths.

When we talk about simplifying, we are talking about conducting all the elements of our lives in concert with our hearts. Moving away from our parents emotionally is important because we have trouble hearing our own heartsongs when our inner ear is tuned to their voices instead.

We need to be able to say, *This is a good choice whether my parents approve of it or not.*

When we cannot, we encounter conflict—with them or within ourselves—over who is in charge. We squander energy trying to make them happy, or feeling guilty or angry because we fall short of the mark.

These conflicts make us feel unsure even about good choices. And they cause us to miss out on what really matters in our adult dealings with our parents: enjoying the best possible relationship with them.

There are two pieces to letting go. One involves how we see ourselves. The other involves how we see them. In emancipating ourselves from fantasies in both pieces, we emancipate ourselves from our parents.

We grow up knowing what our parents wish for us.

We learn this from expectations they voice and expectations they manage to transmit without a word by their example, their criticism, even with a raised eyebrow. However they teach us, we know what they expect.

Many of their expectations are necessary or helpful. They set us firmly on the way to happy, productive adult lives. Others are less useful, rooted in their own thwarted aspirations or painful life stories or tolerance level for letting us make choices on our own.

As children, we have no experience or skills to help us sort the useful expectations from the tainted ones. We internalize them all and set out to live up to them in order to please the grown-ups most central to our existence.

If we never stop to assess the validity of those expectations, we put ourselves at risk to make faulty choices on matters that range from the mundane to the monumental, including our choice of a mate, a career, whether to have children. The possibility of error grows as we ignore our own hearts and defer to theirs.

Unexamined parental expectations also leave us vulnerable to the feeling that we have let them or ourselves down and to all the dark emotions that come with that sensation. We may end up angry with them or full of blame.

We become susceptible to the flawed logic that if *they* would stop expecting so much from us, *we* would feel better. Frankly, if we feel bad when they don't approve a choice, it's a sign that their approval matters more than it should.

Moving away from parents involves replacing the internal echo of their expectations with the internal voice of our own. It also involves letting go of the fantasies that evolved from their expectations.

One of the reasons it is so difficult to let go of our parents' wishes for us is that they are linked to promised results . . .

If you get an education, you'll get a great job.
If you make good money, you'll feel content.
If you get married, you'll be happy.
If you have children, your life will be complete.

It may help us to let go of our parents' wishes if we acknowledge our reluctance to let go of the happily-ever-afters they said would come if we fulfilled them.

In addition to our parents' wishes of us, we grow up with our wishes of them. Letting go involves relinquishing these fantasies, too.

An urbane woman I know has always marveled that she sprang from a mother who, to put it mildly, is on the salty side. My friend would waltz into the living room in pearls and high heels to greet the date who was taking her to the theater and find her mother regaling him with off-color jokes.

For years, she harangued her mother to give up her earthier habits in an effort to create the mother of her fantasies. To both of their credits, the mother refused and the daughter eventually let go of her fantasies. Years later, my friend concluded that her mother had given her something far more important than a sleek maternal model; she had demonstrated the importance of being herself, even under extreme pressure to alter that self.

For the most part, our parents are doing the best they can to navigate their own waters and send us off safely into ours. When they misdirect us, it is rarely from ill intent.

When I ponder why it is so difficult to stop wishing that our parents were someone else, I suspect it is because we still believe that *their* reality is *our* reality, and thus that if *they* were different, then *we* would be different.

Without the astigmatism of false hopes, our vision clears. We can begin to release the sad memories we may have carried from childhood and to unlink our identities from theirs. We can stop clinging to what might have been and blaming our parents for its absence and begin pursuing new, more realistic relationships with them.

That, after all, is where we would like to end up. Parents matter, even to the most neglected or abused among us. When we find a way to keep parents peacefully in our lives, our lives feel more whole.

One of the encouraging aspects of letting go of our parents is that *it's never too late.*

Unhooking our choices from our parents' expectations and seeing them independent of our own are "inside" jobs. Our parents don't have to agree, participate, or even know what we're doing. In the ideal, we resolve our issues in concert with them, but their cooperation is not essential.

As we begin to free ourselves, we make an astonishing discovery: They don't have the same power over us that they once did.

All this time, we've been paralyzed by the same fears that kept us in line when we were five, but it turns out the consequences of letting go at thirty-five are but a shadow of what they were back then.

In fact, most of us discover, our parents only exercise as much influence over our choices and well-being as we grant them. I observed a dramatic demonstration of this truth in a hotel swimming pool a few years back.

A woman and her mother were floating on air mattresses in the middle of the pool when the mother began directing a critical stream of conversation toward her daughter.

"Mother," the daughter softly interjected, "if you keep criticizing me, I'm just going to float away."

The mother promptly changed gears.

Here was a woman who had freed herself from both her mother's expectations and any hope that her mother would change those expectations. She could float contentedly beside her parent, and she could as comfortably set limits when the conversational tide began to drift.

> *Parents can only give good advice or put them on the right paths, but the final framing of a person's character lies in their own hands.*
>
> ANNE FRANK
> *The Diary of a Young Girl*

RITUAL

We know we haven't moved away from our parents when we feel resentful or trapped and find ourselves blaming them for these reactions. We progress in our emancipation when we find ways to reject their expectations while embracing them.

There are three techniques for navigating this stretch of road:

USE VISUAL AIDS.

Find a photograph of your parents when they were young. A wedding photo comes to mind. Occasionally visit the photo and think of your parents in their young married lives—fresh and hopeful and untried, wanting only the best for themselves and for you. This picture may make it easier to be forgiving.

REVISIT HISTORY.

Use the high spots of family as a path to a better place you can share now. Ask a sibling what she remembers about your parents. If they're alive, videotape your parents as they talk about their own lives before your birth, or sit down with them and fill out one of those personal history books such as *Grandma Remembers.* Seek episodes you can share in laughter.

❧ MAKE A LIFE LINE.

On a single sheet of paper, make a time line of your life until now. Note all the major events. Beside it, draw a life line for your parents for the same years. Note the major events of their lives. Compare the two. The discovery that the year you felt so abandoned was the year your mother lost her own parent or the year your father lost his job may help you to gain perspective on how they behaved toward you.

CINDERELLA
HAD IT RIGHT

A friend of mine married a man with two young sons and a hands-off approach to parenting. She worried that the boys would suffer from their father's inattention, so she delivered a steady stream of cards and small remembrances to her husband for signing before she carried them off to the post office to mail to the children, who lived with their mother in another state.

After a number of years, Ann began to tire of the routine. Her husband didn't seem particularly appreciative, and the boys and their father were no closer. She had never been able to forge a close connection with the children herself, and to make matters worse, the boys' mother would occasionally fire off criticisms about the choice of gifts that were sent.

Increasingly, Ann resented the time she spent on what had become an empty and frustrating ritual. She had invented a job for herself, and now it was one job too many.

I meet few women who say that forming a stepfamily has simplified their lives. Stepchildren, ex-spouses, mates and relatives of ex-spouses, ex–in-laws: Each adds another layer of expectations and responsibilities to lives that already have an oversupply of them.

In some cases, step relationships are rich and rewarding. These are cause for celebration. In others, they are less satisfying. Regardless of where our own "steps" fall on this ladder, if in choosing a mate we become stepmothers, we must accept that we have not married a man but an entire tangled network.

As I watched Ann struggle with her stepfamily relationships and as I have since counseled others through theirs, I decided that Cinderella had it right.

Yes, Drizella and Anastasia were awful stepsisters, and here was one stepmother whom the "wicked" shoe fit. But whatever the philosophical flaws of the fairy tale, Cinderella had a personal conviction that she refused to surrender; by declining to buy into her stepfamily's jealousy and cruelty, she kept herself whole.

Stepfamily relationships are innately complicated. Most of us find it hard enough to maintain healthy, happy relationships with the parents, siblings, and children we acquire through birth or adoption. At least with them, we share a common history and, hopefully, a reservoir of goodwill.

With stepfamilies, we don't get the same ingredients of shared backgrounds and experiences. Yet we, or they, may expect the same results.

We can simplify our stepfamily relationships if we begin by sorting out those expectations. What do we expect? What do our husbands expect? What do the children expect? And the mother or father of the children?

It is never too late to say, *Gee, we never talked about this, but*

I'm wondering how you thought it (whatever it is) would work?
Everyone in the family needs to understand the working assumptions of everyone else. When assumptions are in conflict, steps need to be taken to resolve those conflicts.

Because of the profound bonds that tie parents to their children and spouses to one another, stepfamily conflicts may be intense. I have a handful of suggestions as you set out to resolve them.

❧ DON'T LET YOUR FANTASIES GET IN THE WAY OF THE REALITIES.

Sometimes we weigh down our stepfamily relationships with fantasies and expectations that have more to do with our ideals than with anyone else's desires. Illusions that we have to be perfect or to please others or to avoid conflict at all costs are invariably suspect. They can lead us to take on more than we can handle or miss out on ways to make this simpler.

❧ PICK YOUR BATTLES.

With so many people involved, the potential for conflict in stepfamilies is virtually limitless. Everything from religious conviction to how to squeeze the toothpaste tube may clash. You can't fight all of these battles. Draw lines where you must based on what matters most, but don't draw so many that you have no hope of defending the ones that have real importance to you.

❧ REMEMBER THAT "SPECIAL" DOES NOT ALWAYS MEAN "PRIMARY."

Relationships between spouses and between parents and their children are the most precious of life. Each such bond is special in its own powerful and distinct way. In a stepfamily, there will come times when we feel the specialness of one set of bonds competes with—even diminishes—the specialness of another. This is a challenge for the human heart. There's a part of each of us that believes being special means being primary. When this belief sets the agenda for a stepfamily, the life of every member becomes hopelessly complicated.

Because family connections are the most cherished in humankind, they are the hardest to relinquish, even when they are connections we make through marriage rather than birth. Yet sometimes the freight of unhappy histories and unwilling members makes it virtually impossible to achieve the closeness we all hope for in our family relations.

My friend Ann realized that her husband's relationship with his children was ultimately his responsibility. No investment of her own energies was going to overcome his attitudes about being a parent, or the hostility of his ex-wife, or the indifference of the children. She pulled back, dropping not only her mail campaign but other efforts she had made in hopes of creating the close-knit family she had always dreamed of. Her partial withdrawal gave her one less job and lightened the inner load of emotions that the failure to achieve her ideals had created.

Like Ann, you may find that reducing your personal investment in stepfamily relationships is necessary for your family life to remain in harmony with your inner self.

In a world where half of all marriages end in divorce, an estimated one-quarter of all children spend a part of their young lives in stepfamilies. When stepchildren are a fact of our own lives, we want to approach them with high hopes and the best intentions.

At the same time, it may be helpful to keep in mind that

"blended family" is a misnomer. Stepfamilies are more like tossed salads where each ingredient is distinct and identifiable. Different ingredients combine with differing levels of harmony and success.

> *Stepmothering is an art, a survival technique, and an act of giving. . . . Challenging, difficult and usually worthwhile, it either licks you or you lick it.*
>
> CHERIE BURNS
> *Stepmotherhood*

VIII

SIMPLIFYING OUR RITUAL LIFE

KEEPING
THE KIN

In every family, there is typically one member, almost without exception a woman, who emerges as the kin-keeper.

This is the person who remembers the birthdays and anniversaries, organizes the family gatherings, keeps family members current with one another's lives.

Her activities often extend beyond her own birth family. In a marriage, she very likely takes responsibility for maintaining connections with her *husband's* parents and siblings as well.

As our lives become fuller, we have many more connections to maintain and much less time with which to maintain them. The kin who knows, accepts, and loves us can be a marvelous source of encouragement and support. They also add another set of tasks to our already overlong lists.

When kin-keeping is satisfying, it enriches our lives far beyond the effort it requires. When it feels like one more chore, it can threaten the vitality of the relationships involved.

If we yearn to connect with our kin yet find ourselves worn out by the process, it may be time to find a new approach to these activities.

To evaluate the place of kin-keeping in our lives, it helps to start by asking ourselves . . .

Am I the one?

Typically, the nuclear family has a kin-keeper, someone who maintains the links within that family and also acts as a sort of master kin-keeper to keep the unit in touch with all the other units that make up the larger extended family.

In my nuclear family of five, for example, I'm normally the one who makes the telephone calls, writes the letters, or suggests the get-togethers. Within my extended family of parents, three brothers, and one sister, I enjoy a similar role.

When we recognize that we are indeed the kin-keepers, we should periodically check in with our feelings about this role.

Why have we taken on the job? Is it because we value the connections? Or is it because nobody else will maintain them if we do not? Did another member of the family *assign* us the task, or did we initiate it? How do we feel about it now?

In my case, I invest in kin relationships because they matter a great deal to me and because I want to foster extended family connections in the lives of my children. I also tend to be the instigator because I'm the one who moved away, a factor that often increases kin-keeping activities.

For the most part, regardless of how busy I am, keeping these kin is a willing labor of love. If I wasn't so keen on this particular role, however, I know there are ways I could make it simpler.

Sometimes, we make it easy for others to do nothing by failing to ask them to do anything.

I have heard a number of women in therapy complain, *I love my sister (or mother or cousin) and want to be close to her, but I get tired of being the one who always picks up the phone.*

Yet when I ask, *Have you told her how you feel?* they invariably are caught off-guard. It hasn't occurred to them.

Simplifying our kin-keeping can be as simple as having that conversation:

> *I realize that I'm the one who does most of the*
> *calling in our relationship. I enjoy talking with*
> *you, but I'd really like you to do some of the calling.*

Many times, the loved one knows she's been lazy and will agree to shoulder more of the responsibility without much of an argument.

When she doesn't, we may realize we are dealing with someone who doesn't care about the relationship as much as we do. At that point, we need to consider our response.

Personally, I take a long view of these relationships.

Most family members will still be part of our lives long after colleagues, neighbors, and all but the closest of our friends have drifted away.

Knowing this, I make substantial allowances for individual differences. Haven't we all known a wonderful friend or relative who seemed absolutely phobic about penning a note? I certainly do.

I know that Louise from New York does not write letters. That's just Louise, and I know better than to take her aversion to written communication personally. Because she is a friend I don't want to lose track of, I just overlook this quirk.

There also come seasons, especially with elderly relations, when a family member for health or other reasons literally *can-*

not initiate connections. Certainly, this is a time when it is appropriate for us to assume virtually *all* the responsibility for staying in touch.

At the same time, situations do exist that rightly suggest we should question or modify our kin-keeping.

Sometimes, when we are truthful, we find that a connection is more routine than relationship—we long ago stopped enjoying our monthly conversations with Aunt Leonore, but we persist in calling her anyway.

If she's not willing to take over some of the calling, maybe less frequent conversations are in order.

Kin-keeping that comes under the heading of Living Proxy also deserves scrutiny.

I once knew a woman who routinely called her brother, then called her father to let him know what was going on in his son's life, then called her brother back to fill him in on his dad. The men didn't have to bother conducting a relationship with one another. Marianne did it for them—until she figured out that the relationship wasn't benefiting from her stewardship.

On occasion, when we're doing all the work, we can become resentful of kin who don't participate as actively. This is a red flag. Resentment defeats the purpose of the activity. If we can't maintain a connection without feeling resentful and we can't resolve the resentment, there is good reason to question our ongoing investment in it.

In our busy lives, there will be times when, no matter how much our kin matter and how willing we are to take responsibility for our relationships with them, we can't sustain our usual level of communication.

At these times, we need to be honest:

I love you, but I don't have the time right now to call (or write or visit regularly).

The well-grounded relationships will survive. In the meantime, the fallout of our announcement may surprise us. Faced with the alternative of taking more responsibility or having less of a relationship, many among our kin will take more initiative than we or they thought was possible.

We are a family that has always been very close in spirit. . . . [We] are loyal to one another in spite of our differences [and] any rupture in this loyalty is a source of confusion and pain.

JOHN CHEEVER
"Goodbye, My Brother"

COOKIES
CAN
BE BOUGHT

Thanksgiving 1983 is etched forever in my memory.

My friend Roz and I decided to cook the *Gourmet Magazine* Southwestern Thanksgiving dinner from A to Z or, more precisely, from the pickled shrimp and avocado appetizer to the pumpkin flan and pine-nut tarts with cinnamon whipped cream. We started the day before and cooked until midnight. Then I was back at her house on Thanksgiving day at 6:00 A.M. to start cooking again.

By the time we got to the table, we were totally exhausted. The meal itself is a blur, yet I do remember thinking, *It got eaten so fast!*

I'm glad I cooked one *Gourmet* Thanksgiving because it was unforgettable. But most everyone there would have been just as content with turkey, mashed potatoes, and standard pumpkin pie.

I want to go on the record on the side of holidays. Holidays are great. We look forward to them, and we ought to. They bring us together with loved ones and enable us to revisit traditions that connect us with one another and with our histories. Christmas happens to be the biggest ritual event in our home, but the same can be said in other homes for Passover or any other religious, cultural, or personal tradition.

The trouble with holidays in a busy woman's life is that they become the Big Fix. Having somehow survived the rest of the year on hit-and-miss housekeeping and take-out food, a handful of family gatherings and fewer get-togethers with friends, we decide it's time to *catch up*.

We want to make the house sparkle, execute culinary gymnastics for all those overlooked friends and relatives, and perform other feats of holiday derring-do to *make up for* all the things we never had time for the rest of the year.

And we're going to do this, of course, while carrying on all the other zillion tasks we already do every day.

No wonder everything goes wrong.

We invest so much meaning and try to execute so many tasks in such a short period of time that it is probably inevitable we are overwhelmed and sometimes disappointed by the time the major holidays all over.

It's as if, a few weeks before the event, a starter's pistol goes off in our brains, and we are off and running.

We don't stop to sort the traditions that bind us to our faith or our history or our loved ones from the mere habits that we repeat because we always have. We confuse the rituals we perform out of desire with the rituals that are grounded in guilt or questionable obligation.

We lose the perspective to realize that, in an average lifetime, there are only seventy or so Christmas Days or Seders or Thanksgivings and, of these, only a scant few are experienced when our children are young and new to their wonders.

What we need as the holidays roll around is a steel grip on the parts of our traditions that make them meaningful to us and our loved ones and icy indifference to all the rest.

Whole books have been written on how to simplify the holidays, and women's magazines usually start hitting the theme by early fall. I'm going to limit my pitch for simpler holiday celebrations to one suggestion:

> *If you want to create a holiday that's memorable,*
> *it's a good idea to ask the people who matter to you*
> *what they want to remember.*

Most of us don't ask. We just assume that the holidays won't be the same unless we *(fill in the blanks)*. Then we, the rainmakers of holiday magic, set about bringing all those assumptions to life.

So let's start asking, and let's begin with ourselves. After all, if we're going to put on the show, we need to make sure we build something into it for ourselves.

We need to find those traditions that are anchors for our celebrations. When Earline, the friend who checks for blooms, moved into a scaled-down condo too small for a Christmas tree, she knew she had to find a way to have one, even though she is in her seventies and her son is in his forties. Determined, she searched until she found a solution: an artificial half-tree that fit flush against a wall. Tucked against a mirror, it gave the illusion of a whole tree, and her holiday anchor was secure.

Every woman's anchor is different. It's only important to know what it is. For me, a decorated house and our traditional viewing of *A Christmas Carol* are two of them. On the other hand, packages don't have to have ribbons. Christmas cards are not essential—at least for people I'll see anyway—and Christmas cookies can be bought.

If a ritual has no meaning to us, there's only one other conceivable reason to undertake it: because it has meaning to someone we love.

So let's ask them what makes the holiday memorable.

If the family wants turkey, mashed potatoes, and pie for dinner, then let's stop scouring the culinary magazines for alternatives. If our office Christmas party feels like a prison sentence to our mate, let's not drag him along.

Let's poke through the holiday treasure chest and separate the gems from the fakes. We know what we treasure when we find something we can't let go; we know what our loved ones treasure when we find something *they* can't let go. Everything else is an invention, ours or someone else's.

Usually, just figuring out what everyone cherishes simplifies things because they rarely want everything we thought they wanted, and we rarely cherish everything we're doing. Why in the world would we waste ourselves on activities that nobody cares enough about to champion?

And there's a bonus that goes with asking: When holidays are pared down to what matters to them, other family members become more willing to be involved.

Every year, I futilely beg my sons to go Christmas caroling.

This charming tradition has absolutely no appeal to them, so my choice is to give up or go alone.

Yet the same boys consider the tree a must, and they are eager to be involved in decorating it.

Sometimes, when we take the time to discover the longing buried under the holiday frenzy, we find there are better, easier ways to satisfy it.

I know a woman who yearned for a return to the Christmas Eve gatherings of her childhood when her grandparents, aunts, uncles, and cousins gathered for a potluck dinner and gift exchange. After her own children were born, she decided to resurrect the tradition by collecting the cousins and those aunts and uncles who still survived.

It only took a couple years before one frazzled family member, a working mother with three children under five, fessed up that she loved seeing everyone, but the get-together was one event too many in an overbooked season.

The multitude conferred and decided what they really longed for was to reconnect with one another and to give their children a larger sense of family. They agreed that they had chosen a Christmas gathering for nostalgic reasons but that shifting the party to Labor Day would give them an opportunity to connect at a more relaxed time of year. What they gave up in nostalgia, they regained with the leisure to enjoy their time together.

There is also something to be said for the timing of such deliberations. The time to negotiate the turkey stuffing with your husband is not as you are cutting up the celery on Thanksgiving morning. The overwhelmed cousin who opted out of my friend's Christmas party brought up her concerns in the fall, not the week before the event.

Recognizing what is special to us about a holiday and negotiating how we capture it is best done with a running head start.

I have to confess that my favorite holiday is probably no longer Christmas. It's Thanksgiving.

Thanksgiving is not muddied with gift-giving customs. No stores are open. It's not a three-ring circus; it's just uncluttered togetherness, the family or friends getting together and sharing a meal and maybe watching a football game on TV. It is a sacred holiday that cuts across religious lines.

For all these reasons, I am persuaded it is America's most powerful holiday, the one that gets closest to the heart of why we gather to celebrate together.

And, yes, even Thanksgiving is a lot of work—all the extra food, if we're the one cooking, and the cleanup. But, in small doses, I think there is something to be said for days like this, events that break into our routines. We make our Thanksgivings and Christmases and Seders and High Holy Days a big *catch-up* because so much has slipped away.

There's nothing at all wrong with reaching out to recapture some of it. We just need to take care that we reach out for the right things.

> *Ritual—which could entail a wedding or brushing one's teeth—goes in the direction of life. Through it we reconcile our barbed solitude with rushing, irreducible conditions of life.*
>
> GRETEL EHRLICH
> *The Solace of Open Spaces*

THE
BUYS THAT
TIE

One Christmas a few years ago, I received a telephone call to my radio talk show from an obviously distressed woman seeking advice for a particularly knotty gift-giving dilemma.

It seemed that her sister's daughter had embarked on an affair with the caller's husband, which resulted in the husband divorcing the woman and marrying the niece.

Now, Christmas was at hand, the family gathering and gift-exchange were scheduled, and the caller was wondering whether I thought it would be okay if she declined to give a gift to the niece who was married to her ex-husband.

It brought home once again just how symbolic and complicated gift-giving is.

Can you imagine? Here was a woman whose husband had

left her for another woman, a member of her own clan, and she was still fretting about the etiquette of gift-giving.

The ritual of exchanging gifts begins innocently.

As early as preschool, birthday parties are a major event. When we watch the anxious but hopeful face of a four-year-old giver as her gift is opened, we see already the importance invested in a token of our affection. We take cupcakes to school on our birthdays and a present to our teacher on the last day of school.

We figure out early that the gifts we give and receive are affirmations of our relationships. We slip candy hearts into the valentines of all our classmates, but we save the biggest one for our "best friend."

Unlike other aspects of our daily lives, gift-giving isn't something we invent or inherit or have foisted on us by retailers or greeting-card companies. We feel the urge to share from earliest childhood; gift-giving is simply one of the many forms our sharing takes.

The problem is that gifting is a bit like the cute little creature that hatches from the mystery egg in the Steven Kellogg picture book and then turns out to be an offspring of the Loch Ness monster. For most of us, by our thirties, gift-giving has grown beyond the scope of our time, our budgets, and our energy. Our brother's kids have grown up and gotten married and have kids of their own . . . the girlfriend we exchanged trinkets with in college now has a husband, a baby, and two stepchildren . . . the cozy little gift exchange we used to have with our office mate has ballooned to include the whole department.

In fact, a part of why Thanksgiving and Easter are not as

stressful as Christmas and Hanukkah is that they aren't smothered in *gifts*.

And, unlike many other elements of the holidays, gift-giving is a ritual that marches right through the calendar: Every month seems to bring another birth, birthday, anniversary, or occasion marked by a gift.

Far more than men, women are likely to feel weighed down by gift-giving rituals because it is we who buy, wrap, and present most of the gifts. Yet so many times, we find ourselves running the scissors tips through the curling ribbon at midnight, enfolding still another birthday or shower or holiday gift in wrap and bows, and feeling buried under the resulting stack.

Gifts are intended to be the symbols of our love and best wishes. That's why women are so crushed when their husbands forget or ignore birthdays and anniversaries.

Yet if we looked at our own gift-giving habits more closely, we would find at least some of the ritual has shrunken to routine or, worse, a source of anxiety. When the quality or quantity of gifts we give has escalated beyond our emotions or our pocketbooks, we lose the point of the ritual.

When we find a hollowness at the core of our gift-giving ceremonies, it is worthwhile to consider . . .

> *If I could start all over and redesign my gift-giving*
> *rituals, how would they look?*

An honest answer can show us where the weaknesses in our gift-giving customs lie, such as whether we are giving or receiving more gifts than we desire or exchanging them with people whose place in our lives has faded.

Ending a gift-giving tradition is so much more difficult than starting one, so complicated by the symbolism that a gift—or the rejection of a gift—carries. Yet imagine how satisfying it would be to buy and present only gifts we love to people we love.

We can reclaim our gift-giving rituals, but it requires the courage to be direct. We might be able to terminate or avoid gift-giving by simply ignoring an opportunity to give a gift, refusing to kick into the communal kitty, or declining to reciprocate, but it is unlikely we could do so without jeopardizing the connection at the same time.

Those who can simply, peacefully announce to the world, *I don't exchange gifts,* are encouraged to do so. For the rest of us, here are some ways to restore the heart to gift-giving:

1. CUT BACK THOUGHTFULLY.

The good news about cutting back on gift-giving is that so many of us feel the same anxiety about our gift rituals that we are grateful when someone else does the work of giving us a way out.

One friend who decided on this strategy started in October and called everyone on her Christmas list:

> *"I've decided that exchanging gifts has gotten out of hand," she told each one. "This year, instead of giving you and your family presents, I would rather spend the time preparing a meal that we all share together."*

In the case of distant friends and family, she suggested they celebrate their love by pledging to see each other that year or by scheduling a long, sacred phone date rather than by sending gifts.

Without exception, the people she called were relieved. Although the meals she prepared took some time, she reported later, she found entertaining her friends closer to what she wanted from the season for herself and her family.

2. BEWARE OF WHAT YOU BEGIN.

When we make a new friend or meet someone we would like to know better, we often find the impulse to validate the friendship with a token emerging at the same time. At moments like these, we are wise to remember that gifts are like patriarchs in the Old Testament. One begets another.

We can avoid setting off the gift reaction by expressing our affection in other, smaller ways. When we're tempted to buy a gift, maybe we can satisfy the urge with a thoughtful greeting card, presenting a home-baked confection, treating to a coffee date, even springing for the afternoon snack at the vending machine.

Cards, food, and shared moments are tokens of our regard that do not carry the same weight of obligation as purchased gifts. They say *I care* in a quieter way that is often simpler for us to manage and our friends to accept.

3. HEAD THEM OFF AT THE PASS.

Often, we are not the gift initiators; our new friends or neighbors or colleagues are. At moments like this, what is offered is not only a gift but a symbol of proffered friendship. We can accept the hand of friendship without setting off a gift reaction if we watch for opportunities to head gifts off at the pass.

Long before a birthday or holiday, there will be an opportunity to say . . .

I'm relieved that I no longer exchange birthday gifts with my friends. It's made it so much easier to focus on the event. Now we celebrate by spending time together.

Because women regularly talk about shopping, buying, and gifting, anyone who doesn't hear this opening in the conversation isn't paying attention.

After working up the courage for these efforts, we may be dismayed if they are ignored, if a friend, acquaintance, or loved one insists on continuing her gift-giving ritual even though we have made it crystal clear that we wish to modify ours.

At times like this, we need to remember that simplicity lies in bringing our own lives into harmony with what we value. A friend's heartsongs are likely to be quite different from our own. One of the marks of friendship is being able to respect the choices another person makes without having to duplicate them.

Giving presents is a talent; to know what a person wants, to know when and how to get it, to give it lovingly and well.

PAMELA GLENCONNER
English writer

# CELEBRATION

Presenting gifts upon no occasion at all has a way of untying the strings of reciprocation that otherwise might be attached. A gift on an unoccasion simply says, *I love you, and I wanted you to have this because it shows how well I know you and how much I care.*

One friend took the direct approach to preventing her gift-giving rituals from deteriorating into routines. Gifting me on an unbirthday, she said, *What gives me joy is having found this. If you felt you'd have to reciprocate, it would reduce my joy.*

Her announcement enabled her to give freely and me to receive freely.

THAT'S
ENTERTAINMENT

For several years, our family has thrown a Christmas party for neighbors and friends, a huge noisy affair to which everyone brings themselves, their children, and any stray houseguests passing through.

I thought I had simplified the party until one memorable year taught me how much simpler it could be.

We had gone to the mountains the night before the party with plans to come back early to add all the final touches. When my youngest son, Michael, woke up extremely ill, the plans changed unexpectedly.

It was 1:00 P.M. before we got back to Denver. My husband took John and our visiting friends back to the house while I went on to an emergency room. By the time we waited our turn and Michael was examined by a physician who diagnosed acute altitude sickness, the 4:30 P.M. party was in full swing. I returned home in sweats, sneaked upstairs to change, and arrived at the party just in time for the finale: Father Christmas's arrival.

And, as impossible as I would have thought it, everything was just fine. People had pitched in to help. Some things I thought were absolutely essential hadn't gotten done. But the party took place, and everyone had a good time. If they missed anything, nobody said so.

After that year, the party was always easier. It turned out to be like pondering *How many engines could an airplane lose and still fly?* I didn't have to *do* all that I normally did in order for the party to fly quite beautifully.

It's really tempting today to give up entertaining or to transfer it to a site outside our homes.

That's fine when it satisfies our urge to entertain, but many of us long for something more—for the hospitable rituals of opening our doors and bringing friends and loved ones within the fastness of our homes.

We also may be struggling to spend more time at home, particularly if we work at an outside job and have children. We may have children too old for baby-sitters but too young to be left unsupervised. Entertaining, as long as it doesn't send us over the edge, is a way to enjoy our friends *and* our families without leaving the house.

What we need to examine before we rush to the phone with our invitations is . . .

Do I feel a loss when I don't entertain?

If we couldn't care less about entertaining, it's not an activity that makes sense to sign up for.

If the answer is *Yes, something is missing when I don't enter-tain,* we need to follow up with . . .

> *Can I live with the deals that entertaining has to*
> *cut with the rest of my life?*

I remember being a young wife without children and thrilled at the prospect of company for dinner. I would lovingly plan and execute complicated, time-consuming menus.

Today, those events are rare. If we are going to entertain and maintain our sanity, most of us have to cut some deals with reality.

If we hold an outside job, entertaining on workdays is probably out of the question. Entertaining on the other days is possible, but we need to be honest about the limits of our time and energy. I could still put a gourmet meal on the table for guests, but that's all I would get done that week. I can't entertain if it means giving even one weekend day to do it.

The fact is that the norms of hospitality are wonderfully elastic. When people come together because they like one another and want to spend time together, *that's* the main course. When I invite guests to the house, I am frank about what they can expect. If anyone is offended because I serve them a hamburger rather than chateaubriand, I have to wonder what possessed me to ask them and what possessed them to accept.

Entertaining almost always involves food, so if we can manage that part of it, we usually can manage the rest. My strategies for feeding guests have evolved over the years and serve me well.

1. CREATE A FORMULA MEAL.

I have one set of friends who have been to impromptu dinner at my house three times, and I've served them burgers on each occasion. That's my formula "casual" meal. I like it because almost everyone likes hamburgers, they're virtually impossible to ruin, and I can market for this dinner blindfolded. I have other formula meals for occasions when I have more time to plan or when casual won't do.

2. BRING IN THE FOOD.

No longer do we have to settle for fried chicken, cheeseburgers, or tacos. Now we can get drive-through roast turkey and dressing. Almost any taste or occasion can be served with take-out, providing the budget allows. If we factor in the value of the time we need to prepare food and the cost of ingredients, the budget may be more allowing than we thought. Perhaps even a portion of the meal could be brought in to whittle down what we prepare ourselves.

3. ENTERTAIN OUT OF DOORS.

One of the obstacles to entertaining is not the food but the housekeeping. We feel we have to present a clean front to our guests and, naturally, clean up once they're gone. An alternative to this, especially if rambunctious children are involved, is entertaining out of doors. The dusty furniture will still be there, but at least we can't see it from the picnic bench on the deck, and paper plates seem more at home there than on the dining room table.

One friend is never without cream cheese and something tasty to throw over it—clam sauce, green chile jelly, Pickapeppa. She notes that cream cheese keeps eternally in the refrigerator and makes appetizers that are easy but look and taste appealing. Other women accomplish the same goal with frozen appetizers from the local discount warehouse. Entertaining is easier if we approach the menus with the reminder *If it's not simple, I won't serve it.*

When we reduce entertaining to what we can handle, we may find ourselves more willing to tackle it and better able to enjoy it, which is the point, after all.

Although fewer of us throw parties anymore, the same principles work for group entertaining. One of the ways I have simplified my annual Christmas party is by serving *exactly the same things every single year.* My guests have learned what to expect— chicken wings, veggie trays, snacks beyond number, cookies, free-flowing sodas, and mulled cider. This is another secret of sane entertaining: Manage the expectations of guests as well as those of yourself.

Parties offer the advantage of catching up with a number of people at the same time and letting them entertain one another. If we can simultaneously entertain the masses and enjoy ourselves, throwing the occasional party may be more doable than staging small individual dinner parties on ten separate occasions.

Sometimes I think of entertaining—whether for a couple, a family, or a houseful—in the same vein as whistling past the graveyard. When my life seems to have no space for it, inviting friends over has a way of proving that it does. In addition to the social rewards I enjoy, entertaining is my way of spitting at the cosmos and saying, *So there!*

> *A hectic life doesn't mean you should give up your social life. You can always stop at a take-out place that roasts chickens. If people know you're busy, they won't expect a soufflé.*

> DANIELLE STEEL
> Novelist

IX

SIMPLIFYING
OUR
PLEASURES

ONE MOMENT,
PLEASE . . .

One summer's morning, when my middle son, John, was about eleven, we rushed off to the Denver airport and his takeoff for Sibling Weekend at the college where his big brother, Jim, was a student.

It was early in the day, and this was the first of several stops I was scheduled to make. As we wove through rush-hour traffic, I was mentally running through the schedule to figure out how I was going to work everything in. As soon as we arrived at the airport, I deposited John near the complimentary goodies in the airline lounge and headed for the phones to squeeze in a few calls before his flight departed.

Every few minutes, I shuttled back to the seating area to make sure he was okay. Each time, John gave me a personal news update: "Boy, this is the life!" and "You know, Mom, they've sure got some good doughnuts here."

Only after he finally declared with a sigh, "I think I could live here" did I slow down enough to realize how thoroughly my son was savoring what the moment had to offer—a comfortable seat and an endless supply of free doughnuts.

I don't remember what was so important about the meeting I was trying to make or the calls I was frantically dialing, but I do remember how thoroughly John savored those doughnuts.

I know that I resisted telling him not to eat any more and, while he was at it, to get that big leg off the arm of the sofa where it was swinging. I recall that I sat down with him instead of going back to the phones, and that we laughed together and talked and finally said good-bye.

In the years since that morning, there have been many days that felt as full as that one did. Sometimes, in the midst of one, I recall the lesson of the doughnuts and use it to remind me how important it is to be *in* the moment.

My friend Verna, who loves to travel, recalls car trips she took as a child with her father at the wheel. Because he was always more interested in the destination than the journey, she spent these trips with her nose pressed against the car window, longing to stop and actually *see* something other than a motion-induced blur.

Most of us live life the way Verna's father drove the highways, our foot pressed so tightly against the gas pedal that nothing we pass stands out. The moments run together, all of them feeling pressured, with stress the dominant feature in our personal landscapes.

One of the ways we can bring balance to our lives is to *watch* for the moments worth savoring and then to *stop* whatever we're doing in order to savor them.

A moment like the one I shared with John in the airport is not very long. Neither is an embrace or a sunset or the smile on an infant's face when Mommy walks through the door. These won't set back our schedules enough to matter, but they can be a fresh breeze moving through our spirits, softly untangling knots in our souls.

"A little of what you fancy does you good," the English music hall entertainer Marie Lloyd said.

I would add that a little more does you even better.

In the hierarchy of leisure, seizing the moment is a place to start, but it's only a start. In our quest for balance in our lives, we need to revel in every respite that offers itself for our consideration.

Respites take a multitude of forms. They may be solitary or social, passive or active, quiet or noisy. They do not have to be expensive or elaborate; they *do* have to be unhurried, and they must contain an element of *rest*.

My friend Marilyn found a way to incorporate respites into her life that I like to recommend.

One year, she decided she wasn't going to let the holidays get the best of her. In bold marking-pen ink, she wrote a note that read, *December is a gift that I'm giving myself,* and taped it above her telephone.

Every time she was tempted to take on another responsibility or sign up for another activity that month, she looked at the note and asked herself, *Will this feel like a gift?* If she doubted that it would, she resisted.

Marilyn found her message to herself so persuasive that she began to use it on other occasions. I would stop in and find *Saturday is a gift I'm giving myself* taped above the phone, or *Tuesday nights are a gift I'm giving myself.*

Writing down her intention and affixing it at eye level in a place she couldn't avoid was a reminder to herself to make time for respites. They became her permission slips to leisure.

At the top of the respite hierarchy is the most leisurely leisure of all: the vacation. I am a great believer in the healing and saving power of vacations, not only because I enjoy them myself but because of the miracles I've seen them perform in the lives of others.

I see many people in my psychological practice who have pushed themselves so long and so far that they've lost their zest for life itself. Often, these patients believe they can find new meaning in their lives with a new job or a new love or a new home.

Almost as often, I counsel them first to take a vacation, preferably a long one.

The hotel industry's promotions for weekend "minivacations" instead of longer work interruptions pander to our worst impulses. The fact is that we need more than two or three days to disengage sufficiently to recharge low batteries, even if we only get those long respites rarely.

I know a woman who says she's made every major decision of her life on a long vacation. I can see why. Vacations away from home transport us from everything familiar to places where we may not even be able to get the latest world news. They enable us to step back from the canvas and see what we're creating and how much we like it.

A growing number of people take vacations at home, a place where they normally spend so little time that it feels like a retreat. This can renew us provided we are able to smother the impulse to take the time we've carved out of our professional work lives and fill it with domestic work. Home vacations provide us a respite only when they are spent relishing overlooked pleasures rather than catching up on undone work.

Part of the reason we feel overwhelmed by all the balls we juggle is that we have allowed the one labeled "Respite" to fall to the ground. Whenever and however we do it, for a moment or a week, with a plate of doughnuts or a drive through the country, this is one ball that's worth picking up and putting back in play.

> *Were I called upon to offer a formula for "the perfect moment," I might advise to just be where you are—one of the hardest places to arrive at in the here-there-everywhere-at-the-same-time world we've created.*
>
> RODICA WOODBURY
> Associate editor, *Out West* newsletter

CELEBRATION

Research indicates that a pleasant event gives a boost to our immune systems that can persist for as much as two days. In one study, the greatest boost to immunity was found to come from everyday respites such as a get-together with friends or a jog in the park.

When you relax and enjoy yourself, revel in the certainty that your whole body is celebrating and recharging along with your spirit.

TUNING
THE
INNER EAR

A woman I know wanted to learn relaxation techniques for the upcoming birth of her daughter. She considered this so important that she spent many solitary hours in her late pregnancy in practice, which consisted mostly of listening to long, haunting instrumental stretches of the *Out of Africa* sound track composed by John Barry. As she listened, she imagined herself soaring over the African plains.

Ten years after the birth of that child, she says, the melodies from the movie still soothe her. No matter where she is or what she is doing when she hears them, they take her back to that quiet place.

As we seek balance in our lives, it is helpful if we find our own quiet places.

Here in Colorado, many people seek solace in the mountains and streams of the Rockies. Physical remoteness, especially in a natural setting, has always been used by humankind for spiritual renewal.

Yet physical remoteness is not essential. We don't have to go to Tibet for a month to find peace. It exists somewhere within each of us if only we can stake it out.

We find our way to our quiet places on a variety of paths. Meditation, visualization, yoga, and prayer slow the tempo of our lives and free us to hear the whisperings of our spirits. Music, poetry, even running our hands through the moist earth of our gardens, can produce the same inexpressible sense of serenity.

Perhaps the only requirement of a quiet place is that it offers us solitude. Rather like turning off the bell of the telephone, silence is more complete when we know it cannot be interrupted. Solitude lowers the speed, turns down the volume, isolates us from distraction. It is in solitude that we are most likely to hear our inner voice.

Hearing this voice is central to a simpler life. After all, how can we make choices based on what matters to us if we don't know *what* matters to us? Knowing our hearts lets us know what matters, and that knowledge heartens us to let go of the rest.

My friend and associate Jody has an endearing habit that she practices on the telephone.

When an issue she wants to consider without distraction is presented, she will say, "Excuse me. I need to put the phone down so I can think about that."

Then she sets the receiver down and thinks as long as necessary before returning to the conversation.

Jody's custom announces, *This is too important for any-*

thing less than all of my attention, and it enables her to do what she needs to give it all of her attention. It demonstrates a great deal of self-knowledge and the frank self-assurance it takes to act on such knowledge.

Jody uses this technique in conversations. We all need similar triggers in our dealings with ourselves. We need rites that signal to our bodies and souls, *We're in that quiet place again. It is time to relax.*

> *The way we live today requires that we get away from the way we live today.*

AIRLINE MOTTO FROM THE 1970s

FITNESS
IS NOT A JOB
UNLESS YOU'RE
A TRAINER

A few years ago, I read a newspaper article about the transformation of exercise from recreation to work.

It noted that many people who used to work out for the fun of it had added fitness to their "to-do" lists and turned it into another obligation. Of course, once fitness made the list, the story noted, it lost its value as a respite, and people weren't terribly motivated to do it.

What a shame. Exercise is a proven, immediate tonic for stress and depression—a surefire shortcut to simpler lives. Yet we manage to let it make life more difficult.

It is beyond doubt that exercise is good for us. Sometimes it seems as though a day doesn't pass without some snippet of news celebrating the value of exercise.

For women struggling just to get out of the house on time every morning, this is no cause to rejoice.

Oh, great! we groan, *one more thing I ought to be doing and have absolutely no time to do!*

Meanwhile, those who view exercise as a job set our jaws a little firmer and keep on pedaling, jogging, or whatevering with the same grim determination we might take to a root-canal appointment.

I confess: I am not motivated to carve an hour out of *today* in order to live an extra month or two a few years down the line. I'll take the bird in hand, thank you.

Yet I exercise pretty regularly because I found something that overcomes both my resistance and my native tendency to organize every activity into a job.

I have found my own *desire.*

At the back of my yard, in view of my kitchen, runs a century-old canal that winds for eighty-two miles through Denver and beyond. As often as I can, I find my way to the canal path, where I take my own preferred exercise—a brisk walk.

What makes my walks on the canal so renewing is that I am not *driven* to them but *drawn* to them. I know that if I can apply my feet to the canal path for even a few minutes, the rest of *that very day* will be simpler.

Immediacy, I have learned, is the key to my desire.

In my quest for a simpler life, exercise is the one respite that pays me immediate rewards. It propels me physically away from the sources of my stress and slows my pace sufficiently so that I can notice the new buds on the trees or the shade of yellow in the changing aspen leaves. In the midst of physical vigor, my problems pale; in the solitude of exercise, I hear my heartsongs.

When events keep me from walking, I feel cheated. I know I've missed the easiest chance I will get to feel better *today*.

If we are to reap the benefits of fitness, each of us needs to uncover our own *desire* for physical activity, the motivational key that will enable us to unlock the resistance that comes between us and fitness.

Each key is shaped differently for each woman, and some of us rely on different ones at different times.

My friend Jeannette began walking about twenty miles a week when she was in her forties. She lived in a hilly coastal community of California, and she found conquering those hills so demanding that it eased her anxiety about a challenging professional transition.

Over time, Jeannette found that her sense of physical accomplishment spilled over into other areas, including the professional one. Now the career transition is behind her, but she's hooked on exercise for other benefits, including the delicious realization that exercise enables her to indulge her love of food without gaining weight.

If you can't find your own motivational key to exercising, here are some places to look:

IN A TREASURE CHEST

Link your exercise program to a system of self-rewards. *If I work out three times a week for a month, I'm going to reward myself with. . . .* It doesn't matter what the achievement level is or the reward; if you can find something you're willing to work toward, the work becomes lighter.

❧ In missed pleasures

Pair exercise with another pleasure you are missing—listening to music or chatting with a friend who could join you, for instance, but *not other work!* If riding a stationary bike while watching sitcom reruns makes exercise a pleasure, rejoice in your good fortune and start pedaling.

❧ In the facts

Just because they don't do much for me doesn't mean they might not motivate you. So here is a sample of what medical research indicates that exercise improves: emotional balance; physical stamina; resistance to illness, infection, and some diseases; concentration; weight control; sexual satisfaction. You get the idea.

❧ With the kids

If you feel that you don't get enough time with your kids, consider exercising with them. Babies and toddlers can be pushed in strollers, and older kids can keep up on bikes and other wheels. I even know a woman who used her infant—*gently*—as a weight for resistance exercises. If the workout shoe fits . . .

The hallmark of the enduring motivation to exercise, quite frankly, is self-interest: *This is something I do for <u>me</u> because it makes <u>me</u> feel better.*

We are so eager to make commitments to the well-being of others—our families, our friends, our employers, our communities. Exercise is a great place to begin being good to *ourselves.*

If you're one of those women who is already exercising and enjoying it, I need to say nothing else I've written about is worth giving up exercise to make room for.

And if you're not, if you groan at the thought or grit your teeth in the process, maybe rooting through your inner closet for the desire is worth a try.

Those who think they have not time for bodily exercise will sooner or later have to find time for illness.

EDWARD STANLY
U.S. Congressman, 1837–1843

RITUAL

Even when we find our *desire* to exercise, there's still the problem of finding the *time*. If time's the trouble, give one of these remedies a try:

- Walk to work, at work, or home from work.

- Skip the elevator, take the stairs.

- Throw the ball with the dog (or race him for it!).

- Bike or roller-skate with the kids.

- Get up a little earlier and exercise.

- Write physical activity into your calendar *in ink*.

- Walk and talk. Exercising with a friend, a neighbor, or a mate betters your body and your soul.

Or take the information-driven approach to finding time: For one month when you don't exercise, keep score (one to ten) of how well you sleep, how stressed you feel, how anxious you are. If you want, throw in a weekly note on your weight and key measurements. Then implement a one-month trial exercise plan and keep score again. If your scores have gone up with exercise, you may have found the key to your desire.

NOT-SO-SWEET
DREAMS

Sleep. It's been called the "sex of the '90s."

We want it, we fantasize about it, and we can't seem to get enough of it.

Neither men nor women (nor teenagers, for that matter) are routinely getting enough sleep, but women are more deprived than any other population. As many as 40 percent of women over the age of forty may suffer from insomnia, and that doesn't count all the younger women with babies.

It's called a sleep debt, and it comes from chronically getting fewer than the seven to nine hours of sleep the vast majority of us need every single night to be fully rested. Nearly all of us run in the red because sleep is the account we dip into when we are looking for time to do everything else.

The trouble with missing sleep is that it makes our waking hours that much harder.

We are less productive and more irritable, less capable of

handling stress and more likely to get sick. Decisions, efficiency, our sense of well-being, are impaired. A sleep debt can even endanger us. Highway experts have noted an alarming trend toward sleep-related accidents and fatalities on the road.

In our busy lives, it is tempting to seek the time we need for our many responsibilities by cheating on sleep. Yet if we crave a more balanced existence, it may be necessary to increase our investments in the sleep bank.

There are many causes of sleep deprivation. Some people have sleep disorders, which can be diagnosed and treated by a physician. All of us go through periods when work schedules or infants or illness temporarily interferes with our normal sleep cycles. Typically, these pass.

The rest of the time, we have some influence over how much sleep we're getting, but we may need to sell ourselves on the value of using it. As strongly as I feel that each woman must find her own road to a simpler life, I am of the opinion that sleep is *not* an area that we examine by asking ourselves, *Does this matter to me?* Like it or not, sleep matters, and it matters a lot.

Most of us tend to play down the importance of sleep, and as a result, we don't set reasonable limits on our waking hours. When that is the case, we need to find arguments that convince us to go to bed.

It can be enlightening to track how many hours we sleep for several nights running and how we function on the days that follow. If we find that on the days following eight-hour sleeps, we experience fewer outbursts of temper, greater concentration, and superior energy than after six-hour sleeps, we might be more convinced of sleep's value.

Perhaps we would be persuaded by tracking our sleep

habits and comparing them with how those around us elevate our outlook and energy levels. We can count on the bleachers to notice when an edge has crept into our voices.

Maybe we just have to say to ourselves, *I know this is important, and I'm going to do something about it.*

To upgrade sleep as a priority, it helps to expose what is keeping us awake.

Some women rob their sleep accounts to wash clothes or do the grocery shopping. Many of us rob them for work. Caffeine and alcohol are crutches we use during the day to perk us up and in the evening to slow us down, but both end up interfering with our sleep.

Getting more sleep may require some negotiating—with ourselves, our mates, our families.

One working mother I know always read for relaxation in the quiet hour after her children went to bed. As her children grew older and had later bedtimes, her "quiet hour" got later and later until it encroached on her sleep. For a while, she kept up her reading because she enjoyed it and she cherished it as a respite.

Eventually, however, she noticed that the quality of her waking hours was deteriorating. Reluctantly, she cut back her nighttime reading. In her self-negotiations, she realized that sleep was more necessary to her balance and well-being than this particular pleasure.

Even respites are not worth losing sleep over.

When household chores are behind our sleep debt, we may be able to use that to negotiate for help.

We might point out to our children . . .

*I get grouchy with you because I'm tired. If each of
you would make your own lunch, I could sleep
fifteen minutes longer in the morning, and I
wouldn't be so irritable. All of us would be better off.*

(If nobody steps right up to enlist, I'm not above saying, *I need
another fifteen minutes' sleep, so someone else needs to make the
lunches.*)

We may need to be more inventive about the timing of our
domestic chores.

Do clothes *really* have to be removed from the dryer the instant it stops? Or couldn't we throw them in and go to bed, letting them dry while we sleep before pulling them out in the
morning? If that bothers someone else in the family, maybe
you've found a candidate for dryer duty.

And there has to be an alternative to the midnight shopping
escapades that 24-hour supermarkets encourage. Some women
throw coolers into their cars so they can do grocery shopping on
their lunch breaks and sleep at night. Almost any arrangement is
better than sleepwalking through the grocery store.

When we live with people whose sleep needs are different from
our own, these differences are not merely amusing. He or she
who sleeps least determines to a large degree how much sleep
everyone else gets. The newborn is pretty obvious in her influence, but the husband who routinely crawls into bed an hour
after we do or crawls out an hour earlier has a similar impact.

Solutions to body-clock variations range from earplugs to a
pact that the mate who sleeps least dresses and undresses in another room. Whatever the solution, negotiations are in order.

The sex-sleep connection also merits exploration. Women

married to night owls often complain that when they do get to bed on time, they are awakened by husbands who come to bed later and expect to find a playmate. This pattern doesn't promote good sleep or good sex and requires negotiation or both will suffer.

My friends Mary Beth and Bob rewarded themselves after a particularly hectic winter with a vacation to a Caribbean island. For the first two days, they did little but sleep. For the rest of the week, they slept less but still far more than normal.

After a few nights, both realized that their sleep was characterized by wild and vivid dreams, and they looked forward to waking up every morning and comparing nocturnal adventures. It was as if their subconscious minds had been buried under their workaday routines and were only percolating to the surface in the luxury of abundant sleep.

In a way, they were right. Dreams are thought to be one of the ways we sort out our waking experiences. When we don't ever sink into the deep sleep that enables us to dream, we miss out on an important sorting time and the emotional balance it nurtures.

The importance of sufficient sleep cannot be overestimated. Find a way to reinstate sleep, and everything else in our lives becomes easier to simplify.

> *"Lord Jesus Christ, have mercy and save me! Let me lie down like a stone, O God, and rise up like new bread," Platon prayed, and turning over, he fell asleep at once.*

> LEO TOLSTOY
> *War and Peace*

CONCLUSION:
KEEPING
IT SIMPLE

It has been several years since my visit to the Amish wood-worker's home. Nonetheless, if I knocked at his door today, I am certain I would find little changed.

Despite the passage of years, his rooms would be unclut-tered, his walls unadorned. He would appear older, no doubt, but his manner would still have the quiet assurance that comes from anchoring life with what is most important.

A few Music Men hawking another way of life might have passed his way since I met him, but I can't imagine that he bought their wares. He has known his heart too well and too long to be easily seduced by false promises.

Those of us who are newer to living in concert with what we value most highly may not find it so easy to maintain the simplicity we achieve. We listen to our heartsongs, we catch the tune, we bring our lives into harmony, and then we may find . . .

> *The silence and open spaces we have created in our efforts to simplify feel a little empty.*
>
> *Old familiar habits and patterns beckon us back.*
>
> *The popular ethic urges us to* <u>*keep up! be accessible! make every minute count!*</u>

The telephone rings with a request we want to reject and yet we think, *But I have so much more time now. I could say* Yes *just this once.*

And so, if we're not careful, we begin anew—adding the loads and the layers we worked so hard to reduce.

In her wonderfully friendly gardening manual *The Garden Primer,* Barbara Damrosch warns readers, "Unfortunately, in the very act of weeding, you make it possible for new weeds to grow."

The same may be said for the simpler life.

Whether we clear out the closet or weed our friendship gardens, travel a few steps or many miles down the road to a simpler life, simplifying our lives creates *space.*

Instead of feeling hemmed in by responsibilities, relationships, and just plain *stuff,* a simpler life gives us elbowroom for our bodies and our souls. We feel freer and calmer. Wise choices are easier to spot, and life feels increasingly balanced because we make more of them.

As we luxuriate in our newfound space, however, we need to be mindful of how we restock it. The same thoughtful approach we used when we reconsidered and revised our old, cluttered lives needs to be brought to our new, uncluttered ones.

We want to beware of what I think of as "soul weeds"—all those questionable choices that trespass upon our spirits and take up our time, energy, and space without renewing and enriching us. When we find one springing up in the space we've worked so hard to create for ourselves, we need to consider the newcomer through the prism of what matters to us and be sure we want to encourage its growth.

Thankfully, as we have cleared the space in our lives that gives new possibilities room to present themselves, we have gained some confidence and skills in spotting what doesn't belong. We have developed courage to turn away requests and learned words that enable us to exit from undesirable situations with relative grace.

We will occasionally err. No matter.

As long as we listen to our hearts and honor the songs that we hear, we remain headed in the direction we chose—on the road to a simpler life.

ABOUT THE AUTHORS

ANDREA VAN STEENHOUSE, PH.D., was Denver's leading radio psychologist for twelve years. She continues to make frequent appearances as a highly visible expert on matters of the heart, soul, and life.

DORIS A. FULLER is a former award-winning journalist for the *Los Angeles Times*.